Who Am I Anyway?
Why Am I Here?

Bobbett Bettencourt

Roky,
Plant a Seed
Everyday!

☺

Love,
Bobbett
2012

Dedication

I dedicate this book to my beautiful niece and godchild, Tanya. For I believe she has never felt special, and today I am telling her that she is and always will be to me. Also to my grandson, Mason. You are just a young boy at the present moment, but I know that God has already called you to serve. Your heart is pure, and it shows in everything you say and do. Remember, Mason, Grandma will always be with you. Last but never least, this book is being dedicated to all who suffer from something called an addiction. My heart is with you.

**Anguish of the addict,
the addict only knows
sorrow for its existence.
Cries for His mercy.
Praise of His holy name,
Lord Jesus Christ**

Contents

Preface

This is a true story. Much of it was very painful and difficult to write, but I felt compelled to do so as God guided my hands. I would sit in front of my computer and pray that God would give me the grace, the courage, the insight, and the wisdom to write so that if just one individual read my story that they will somehow get it or understand what I am trying to say. I prayed that they might awaken from their slumber and live in the *now,* the present—the single moment that you are living right now. Because there is nothing else but this moment, and in *my* moment, I choose to share with you.

This story was not written to assign blame or embarrass anyone. I have nothing but love towards all members of my family and harbor no wish to hurt anyone unnecessarily.

Therefore, I have changed some of the names or left names out to respect and protect the ones I love. This story is about me, but you have a story, too, so really it's about you and not about me. The message here goes much deeper than my life experiences. It's an opportunity to awaken to your life purpose…and to forgive your-self, forgive others, and let this day be the day you make a difference in someone else's life.

Acknowledgements

First, I would like to thank my Father in heaven for giving me this experience on earth. I'm so grateful for being born into this world and to have the opportunity to live, breathe, and share with others.

I thank my Grandpa Bettencourt for being the brave young man he was, to have sailed across the ocean from the Azores to the Americas for a better life.

I thank my Grandma Bloomer for always looking me in the eyes and seeing me for me…and loving me anyway!

I thank my dad for teaching me to be strong and never give up. To stand for what you believe in and be proud of who you are. Rest in peace, Dad.

My mom, for giving me life and loving my dad. Also for being there when I needed you—I know it wasn't easy at times. I pray I wasn't too much trouble for you.

I thank my sisters and brother for being there for me in times of trouble and peace. Brenda, thank you for being my big sister. We all need one to keep us in line. I wish it could have been more. But we still have time.

Balinda, thank you for always listening and seeing me for who I am. And for never judging me. I love you for that.

To my fourth sister, thank you for everything we experienced together as sisters. I love you so. I will never forget all the good and bad times you, Benni, and I had together as kids. They are all cherished memories!

Benni, thank you for being my baby sister. You have brought so much joy to my life. You and me, just like peas and carrots forever.

To my brother, thank you for being the man you are. Solid like a rock, just like our dad. You remind me so much of him. I pray that we may always have a strong bond together and nothing shakes it.

I thank my sons, Michael and Mitchell, for giving me the best experience ever—being your mom. I love you both so much!

Michael, thank you for just being who you are—always such a loving soul. You are one who cares so much for others. I love your hugs—never stop giving them to me. You are one of the best things that ever happen to me!

Mitchell, thank you also for just being who you are. You have made me smile more times than I could ever count. You have always been such a good boy and have grown into such a wonderful man. So independent—not a crowd follower. I'm proud of you for that. You are one of the best things that ever happened to me also.

To my most precious husband, Marlin—thank you for choosing me. For loving me. For believing in me. For giving me two perfect sons. And for growing together, side by side, for all these years. You truly have been the wind beneath my wings. For all the experiences that the Lord has given to us, good or bad—I wouldn't have wanted to do it with anyone else but you. Thank you again for helping me become the person the good Lord intended me to be. I love you, Honey!

Acknowledgements

Thank you to all my friends and family who have loved me, stood my by side, and put up with me. I love you all for that.

Thank you to my good friend, Pastor Ralph Etharidge. For the Lord spoke to him, and in faith he chose to follow his heart and gave a message to me so I could serve God, my Savior, all the days of my life.

I would also like to thank Dallin Larsen and all the wonderful people in MonaVie for bringing one of the most amazing products ever to market and for his faith in God to see it through. As the world can now see, you definitely have a winner here. We are so thankful to be part of it.

I must also give a big thank you to my friend Cheryl Henderson. Without her belief in me, you would not be reading this book. She is one of those people who reached out and touched me, for she walks with the fruit of the Holy Spirit. She helped me see that I do too. I am forever grateful she took the time for me.

And one last thank you goes to John Mason and Michelle Mason for helping me get this book in print and out to everyone who needs to read this story.

Thank you. Thank you! I'm forever grateful to you all. Thank You, Jesus!

Introduction

I'm just a simple country girl who always wanted more…and I knew I wasn't getting it. By "more," I mean, specifically, regarding love. I watched TV—I saw how people loved one another, and nothing like that was going on in my home. I looked at those around me and often wondered why they acted the way they did.

They never looked me in the eyes, never really saw me or asked me what's going on inside. I grew up that way.

My parents loved me—I know this for sure. They gave me food, shelter, and clothes. But they never gave me the nurturing I so desperately wanted and needed.

I'm sure a lot of us grew up that way. It's made us the strong people we are today.

But during it all, I was lost and full of fear…so lost that, at times, I gave up on God. I figured that it had to be a big lie they were telling me.

It didn't make sense. You can't tell a little girl that there is this Spirit in the sky called God. He

Me

created this whole earth for you and me to live in because He loves us so much...and then turn around and not see *me* for who I *am.*

I didn't trust that.

I was afraid. And all my fear kept me asking two questions: "God, who am I?" and, "Why am I here?"

Those answers would be revealed to me because God is faithful...but not until I experienced a full-fledged drug addiction.

The question I would like to know the answer to is if I had been loved and nurtured in a more positive way, would I have still become a drug addict? My grandmother on my mother's side was an alcoholic. Was my addiction hereditary? Or was it that the world was not making any sense at all and I just wanted something that made me feel better than what was being offered?

Drugs were an escape. But when I could no longer hide behind the drugs, at the age of thirty-one, I became exposed. Exposure led me into a drug rehabilitation program.

In drug programs, you are asked many questions about yourself. I was ready to give up on the drugs...but not so ready to share my pain with total strangers. They could not possibly understand what I'd been going through.

My understanding of a lot of things was pretty much out of whack. But through a twelve-step program, great counselors, and a death-do-us-part husband, I was able to draw close to a higher power, that being my Lord and Savior Jesus Christ.

Being raised Catholic, I never had a close personal relationship with Jesus. I never understood the dynamics of how much He really loved me. Or what He wanted me to do for Him.

I started writing this book over fifteen years ago. But I stopped at the second chapter. God has now revealed to me why—I needed to experience what humiliation was: a total surrender of myself to

Jesus. I needed to humble myself before God and allow the Holy Spirit to come and give me peace. I had to throw in the towel and let go of the pain as the Spirit revealed to me that I was never to run the show.

The Lord took this heavy heart and showed me the way.

This is my story: one of tight bonds, fear, hard work, true love, addiction, and—with God's help—recovery and discovery of my true self.

If I can help just one person with the understanding that God loves you and I love you—even if you are a drug addict or so deep in your pain that you see no way out—then my experiences take on greater meaning. There is a way out!

You hold so much value. You just don't know it yet…*yet* being the BIG word here. As I like to say, it's only that you don't know what you don't know.

Hey, we all fall. It's not the drug that makes you a bad person: It's the state of mind that you carry around with yourself…a big fat lie. Someone lied to you. They probably didn't mean to….

They didn't know either.

So, for those of you reading this who need to think beyond what's in front of your own two feet, I would like to challenge your thinking. Go deep inside yourself. Start asking God, "Who am I, and why am I here?"

Let God show you. He will be there to help you through it all.

It's scary at first, but as you roll back all those pictures and memories together, your thoughts will start getting clearer and clearer—crystal clear.

Let's love everyone unconditionally. Let's show everyone respect and dignity, compassion, and forgiveness. That's how Christ gets it done. I'm following Him!

Praise the Lord all day long. It's a new day with air in my lungs. Celebrate that!

Knowing

Who knows the depth of one's soul? Only God knows the answer to that question. When I search my soul, I find it too complex to be able to speak easily to anyone about it. I have found through my experiences only a small number of people here on this earth's plain know who they really are; or they are too confused by religious teachings to know the truth about one's own self.

As I have ventured through this life, my question to my Lord has been, "Who am I? What am I here for?" In searching for those answers, it has been revealed to me that I am here to love and bring comfort to all who come my way. That's it.

Isn't that simple? Not so easy, though, when others have not found their true selves. They roam this earth most of their lives, confused because they have not come to the threshold of knowing.

And what is the threshold of knowing? I don't sit here saying that I know everything there is to know about this journey on earth—but I can say I have found what true happiness is...true joy.

I have heard this question from people along the way in my life: "How do you become a happy and peaceful person?" I can tell you this: It's knowing—when you know that you know.

But how do you know?

It's not easy for the confused and brokenhearted.

It takes patience.

In this body that my spirit wears, somewhat tarnished and half-broken, I find contentment even knowing that my earthly life is close to the end. I'll rejoice in the release of my flesh. It's not quite done yet. There is more for me to do. But when my life is cut from this earth, please do not be sad. I'll be in a place waiting for you, all that I love.

My true wish in sharing all God has put in my life is for you to ask the question, "Who am I?" And let the answers come as you open your heart to the truth.

God will give you all that you search for. Always thank Him for things you have not seen or heard, understanding that all will come by knowing it has already been done for you. It's believing that thought that gets you there. We don't try to make the flowers grow, the wind blow, or the sun shine. It just does.

Patience—always patience—in knowing it's already done.

Bobbett Bettencourt

2004

Chapter 1

First Thoughts

One of my earliest memories is lying on my bed at the precious age of five, trying to figure out how to get my way. It was my first day of kindergarten, and I wasn't so sure if I really wanted to go.

Mommy told me that everything was going to be OK. But, I wasn't sure if I believed her. I thought maybe she just wanted me out of her hair. She didn't pay much attention anyway. Or maybe she needed some peace of mind. I don't know; at the time she did have five daughters, all under the age of eight, to take care of. I'm sure that it wasn't easy for her, considering she was only twenty-six years old.

Somehow, I just couldn't swallow that she was throwing me out of the nest, so to speak. I liked being in the nest. It was comfortable there. I had all my sisters to play with. I didn't need anyone else telling me what to do and how to do it.

As I was pondering all of that, before I knew it, my mother came into my room. She got me off my bed and started searching my closet for the pretty new dress I was to wear. I figured I'd let her have her way this time, since I had a new dress to wear. Those didn't come along that often.

My mom and sisters. The Nest.

As we walked onto the schoolyard, I saw all kinds of kids that were the same size as me—well not quite; I was pretty small for my age. (I remember my mother taking me to the doctor all the time, because she was concerned that I wasn't growing. I just didn't grow much.)

School looked like it might not be so bad. New faces were everywhere—and so many people to talk to and play with. This might be fun.

Like most children, I viewed my world as one big playground. My playground was full of curiosity, wonderment, and fear. Oh yes, and cows, too.

My curiosity led me to wonder why I was always so afraid of parents who were supposed to love me. Their version of love didn't match mine. I didn't understand why they were mad most of the time. Was that love? I loved my parents, but I didn't understand why they didn't show me that they loved me the way I understood it.

I was confused most of my life, always wondering, "Who am I, and why am I here?" "Are people always going to be mean to me?" "Is there another way to live, except in fear?"

"Will I ever be good enough for someone to *really* love me?"

When I was a little girl—six or seven—I remember standing out in the hall, in the middle of the night, all alone, because I was afraid of the dark. The light was on out in the hall, but I couldn't see out there. Everything was fuzzy and blurry. No one knew I couldn't see yet. I didn't even know I couldn't see. But I knew I was afraid.

I was afraid of my dreams. Afraid to leave closet doors open for fear something might be in there. Or that there might be something under my bed that would get my feet. Or how about placing a perfume bottle next to my bed so I could spray an intruder in the eyes? I was afraid. What can I say?

I know most children have bad dreams. And I've often wondered why that has to happen. It seems so cruel. But I guess that's just all part of it.

I had spooky dark dreams that went forever, with big old creepy overhanging trees, which dwarfed me. Their branches were like arms. They were all trying to grip at me at once. I couldn't get away.

I awake, struggling. Afraid. Trembling.

I climb out of bed.

Go to the light. The hall has light.

I look down to the end of the hall where my parents' bedroom was. It seemed a mile away.

I walk to their door.

It's closed…as always.

I stand there, scared.

Should I knock? I knock lightly.

I hear a rough voice…my dad. "What?"

"I'm scared."

"Go back to bed."

"But…"

"GO TO BED!"

That's loud, and it hurts.

Now I'm even *more* afraid.

I walk back—back to my place in the hall. The place I knew so well.

No one knew how scared I was.

No one seemed to care.

I had many nights in that hall, wondering why I was sitting out in the hall in the middle of the night and no one was around to comfort me. I realized my life was going to be about fear.

There wasn't anything to do but sit there and think, but sometimes I would get energetic and clean out the sock drawer that stood in the hall. It was usually pretty messy (many days, I went to school with socks that didn't match) with five girls digging for a pair of socks that matched every day. So I figured I'd clean up the mess, which left me the best pick. Smart, huh?

There wasn't much to do, except be afraid. So I would wake my sisters up on purpose, so I wouldn't have to be afraid alone. They'd tell me to go back to sleep.

But I couldn't go back to sleep—too many ugly things in my dreams. Remember, the trees were going to get me.

Maybe that's why I was such a small, sneaky, mischievous child—I wasn't getting the proper sleep. My mind was running wild with fear. I was afraid at night, and the days were no better. I was afraid of my dad. He was mad a lot. (Or it seemed at the time anyway. I believe my sisters can vouch for that.)

That's why it's extremely bizarre, knowing my dad had a hot temper, that I would do something intentionally, knowing I was going to get in trouble over it. Back in the sixties, ottomans were the thing. My mom was proud of her shiny new orange vinyl ottoman…until I took a butcher knife to it. *Why would I do that?*

I remember the actual act. It felt good sticking the knife in a solid object. I'm not saying I'm a psycho. But apparently something was going on in my head.

"Hey! Look at me."

"See what I'm doing."

"I'm punching holes in your new ottoman."

"Can I get in trouble, please?"

And in trouble I would get... But that didn't stop me.

I remember my mom receiving a nice expensive bottle of perfume...Chanel N°5 as a gift from my dad. I locked myself in the bathroom and squirted the whole bottle down the sink.

What is wrong with a child who does things like that?

I wanted attention so badly! I wanted to be loved like the people I saw on TV. So, maybe if I act like the kids on TV, they'll pay attention.

The Brady Bunch seemed like a good family to copy. I'll be Jan, the middle daughter. Always be a good girl. Get good grades. Don't bother anyone. Don't speak unless you're spoken to. Stay clean. Smile. And pick your lunch up on the way out the door to school, which the housekeeper made especially for you....

Hey, wait a minute. We don't have a housekeeper! And I didn't get a homemade lunch. I ate the hot lunch in the school cafeteria—tamale pie with corn in it was the worst. It was this hunk of orange gritty mush. It was awful. It looked like dog poop.

I would look over to the kids with the cold, homemade lunches and wish I had a peanut butter and jelly sandwich.

No, life didn't seem quite fair. Orange tamale pie, creepy old trees, work every day, and no one seemed to care.

No one asked if I liked the crap they served in the cafeteria or why I stood at the door knocking in the middle of the night.

No one asked.

My fear led me into all kinds of things, good and bad. Mostly bad. But the sad part was that no one was paying any attention— *really not paying any attention.* I didn't feel special to anyone.

Except possibly a voice out of the sky. Was I crazy? What did I hear?

I was brought into this world on a hot July day, way back in 1958...born to a young, good-looking couple. My parents had six children—five daughters and one son. The girls came all in procession, one through five. We are a year apart from one another. Then five years after the last daughter was born, finally came the son they so desperately wanted.

I was raised on a dairy farm. With that came a lot of responsibilities. I remember working at a very early age of about seven or eight. As soon as I was able to carry a bucket of milk, I had a job. Seven days a week, 365 days a year. You didn't get off unless you were sick...and you had to be almost dying. You know, throwing up, 104 temperature, can't get up kind of sick. And you knew you better not fake it!

My sisters and I fed calves twice a day—in the morning before going to school, and as soon as our feet hit the ground as the bus dropped us off around 4:00 p.m. So, in the winter months, you hardly had any time before it was dark.

I hated the dark. I was afraid. So I had to hurry.

It was hard work to load heavy cans of milk up onto the back of a pickup, get to your destination, and train newborns to drink from a bucket or a bottle. Those little things were stubborn, and some calves were much stronger than me! It took a lot of muscle. But we all stood the test of time. Common sense told us how to take care of a living animal. You must love them, even if it's just a calf.

My sisters and I would always get into fights about what each of our responsibilities included. Maybe I was just too bossy, but an incident happened when one of my younger sisters got mad at me, probably for telling her what to do.

Back in the late sixties, we didn't have much. And that went for how we fed the animals too. We had an old—and I mean old—top-loading washing machine in which we would mix up the milk and a powder substance, called milk replacer, with cold and scalding hot water.

There was a hose attached to the washing machine to fill the bottles with the milk mixture. As I remember, we had to wear rubber boots, because it was always wet in that area where we prepared the bottles, and that old washing machine had no electrical ground. And sometimes, if you weren't careful, you'd get shocked.

So, on this particular day, my sister and I got into an argument as she was filling the washer with the scalding hot water. Apparently, she didn't take what I said very kindly…and before I knew it, I was being sprayed in the face with the hose she had in her hands. It was the scalding hot water. I'm surprised I'm not scarred today from that attack.

As my surprise left me that she could even do such a thing, I stood there soaked from head to toe, my skin burning. I looked up to see my sister laughing hysterically at the looks of me. I guess I never meant that much to her or the way I looked was just too funny.

Working and living side by side on a dairy with my sisters and brother created a strong bond that will never be breached. We may not see or speak for days or months, but we all know without a shadow of a doubt if any one of us ever needed anything, all we'd have to do is call and we'll be there.

Looking back on my childhood years, what I remember most was always being in trouble for one thing or another. It seemed my dad was always in a bad mood. This made it extremely tough for me because I've never been a person who gives much energy into being mad. I didn't see the point in it. It's simpler to be happy. I'm not saying I had a really bad childhood—there were some good times—but it was very difficult.

When I think of my childhood, floods of memories come into mind…memories of good times playing with my sisters and brother, being around all the cows and hiding and dancing and being free in the cornfields. Playing with our dogs, Happy and Toby. Happy was a female German Shepherd and Toby was her son. How my sisters and I loved our dogs! They followed us everywhere, for they were our protection.

There are a lot of good things to be learned while growing up on a dairy. Our father taught us a strong work ethic from his diligence. I didn't know he was teaching me these things at the time. He probably didn't either. There were a lot of dangers to think about on a daily basis. So being careful took some ingenuity from our precious little minds.

There was one time that calves just kept dying. I would treat them with medicine and nurture them with my love. But they kept dying anyway. Every time a calf would die, I would get into trouble.

So one day this calf dies. I was so afraid to tell my dad another calf was dead. I knew if I told, I wasn't going to be able to go to my best friend's birthday party, so I didn't tell him.

I just left it in its pen. In a few days, they start to rot. If it's hot, it happens sooner. Of course, there are a lot of flies on a dairy. And flies lay eggs that turn into maggots. I didn't know what I was thinking; I knew my dad would be checking on us every few days.

When he discovered the remains, all you could see was the maggots moving underneath its hide. My dad was so mad at me that he told me to get in that pen and drag it out. But when I pulled on its leg, it almost came off. I had to get a shovel to get that calf out of there. Not a pretty sight…shoveling pieces of calf remains.

Can you imagine what that experience could do to a child at such a tender age? I was devastated to say the least. I'll never forget that. But as much as that might have scarred me, there is another story that cut even deeper.

I was fourteen. The day had been one wet, dreary storm after another. I got off the bus from school, changed my clothes, and got to the milk barn. I went through my daily rituals to get started feeding—filling the milk cans, loading them on the Bronco, the vehicle we used to get down to the feedlot where the calves were half a mile away.

I finished filling the cans with milk and made my way down to the feedlot and got started as usual. A few minutes later, here came my dad ranting and raving about calves being out of their pens. They were running around everywhere. So, I had to stop what I was doing and go put these calves back in their pens. Mind you, it's a cold, dark, stormy night.

My cousin and my two younger sisters were there also. They helped me get them back in. There was one calf that was definitely too big to go back in that small pen. I was trying to put a 200-pound animal in an opening of about four feet high by three feet wide. The calf would not go in.

My dad kept yelling at me to get it in. But it just wouldn't go in. It was too big to fit. I was cold, wet, and frustrated and felt like I had no value at all at that moment. I was so angry by this time that as soon as the calf got close enough to me, I gripped it around the neck and bit it as hard as I could. When I let go, to my surprise, that damn calf finally went into that pen, scraping the hair off the back of his neck as he made his way in! I had hair all stuck in my teeth. It tasted awful. When I looked up, there were my cousin and my sisters laughing so hard that I thought they would pee their pants. Later, I found out, they did.

What a sight that must have been. I'm sure I would have been laughing about it if it had been someone else but me. But it wasn't. I will never forget that night as long as I live. Believe me when I say, they'll never forget either. To them it was funny...something to laugh about. But that night, I lost something—the value of self. I was no one to anyone.

I was mad at my parents for being so mean and not looking at me or taking time for me. I was mad at the world. It had no peace. It seemed everyone was mad about something. I couldn't handle all the anger and pain. My frustration was *beyond* frustration.

At fourteen years old, my life started in another direction. This little Catholic girl stood at her breaking point.

They taught me about a God who is supposed to love me, taught me to go to church, sometimes say a prayer or two, give some money, and leave your sins at the altar.

But they treated me like I didn't matter at home. I didn't get it.

Some people didn't look *through* me, like my Grandpa Bettencourt and Grandma Bloomer. It seemed I didn't get to have them for very long. They were only loaned to me for a short time, and then they were gone. I missed them so much. There is also my beautiful godmother, Jackie. She is truly an angel. These people stand out.

I would say these people looked at me and cared. They didn't look *past* me.

My Grandma and Grandpa Bettencourt lived down the lane, half a mile away from our house. My seven cousins also lived down the lane. My sisters and I would walk down the dirt lane or travel through the cornfields to Grandpa Bettencourt's house.

There were sections in the cornfield that the corn didn't grow. My sisters and I would take these vacant pieces of property and set up camp. We would play for hours in the corn with our protector Happy and all her pups. We would play house and pretend the puppies were our babies.

Then we would stop by the giant silos that stood behind the barn and the corral that housed a beautiful horse named Beauty. She was so tall—one of the tallest horses I've ever seen to this day. My sisters and I would bring her treats. She knew we'd be coming, for she heard the rustling in the corn coming her way. She would be standing by the fence waiting patiently for her treat.

As we would make our way to Grandpa's house, we'd walk by their fishpond. It wasn't very big, but to a small child it seemed like a lake. We'd stop for a minute or two to catch a glimpse of the goldfish.

My grandparents' home was very small. It was built sometime in the early 1900s, and that house still stands today. As we walked through the porch, there was always a big bag of dog food, and my sisters and I would sneak a bite. We thought it tasted good! But it didn't taste as good as the round flower-shaped vanilla cookies my grandfather would give us.

At my Grandpa and Grandma Bettencourt's, age 5.

It was always my grandfather giving of himself. I can still hear him asking us in his best effort to speak English, "Do you want a cookie?" My grandfather knew how to speak English, but it was with a very strong Portuguese accent.

We all said yes. Then I would hear my grandmother yelling from the living room, "Don't let those kids come in here with those cookies!"

My grandmother, as always, would be sitting on the couch knitting or crocheting. She wasn't a very affectionate woman—and that's being kind. I got the hint. She didn't like us. But that's because she didn't like my mother.

My poor mom…she always got the nasty end of the stick when it came to her in-laws. My grandfather was decent to her, but grandma was downright rude.

I remember my grandfather picking us up in his old green Studebaker for church on Sunday mornings. All five of us would pile in the backseat. It was huge back there. Grandfather had a very close relationship with God. He was a very faithful Catholic man. His religion was a sacred thing, and it showed in everything he did.

He came over on a ship from the Azores in the early 1900s as a young man all by himself—only two months shy of his eighteenth birthday. What a brave young man. He told us he saw a lot of people die on the voyage over to the United States.

He reached the port of San Francisco and found a job on the docks until he saved enough money to travel east. He settled in the small town of Hilmar, about ninety miles from San Francisco. There was plenty land to be had. He found six hundred acres of open ground. That is where he started a dairy and raised his family. My father was the last born of three children, and he had two older sisters.

With my grandfather, there was always time for storytelling. We would sit at his feet as he rocked in his chair, twiddling his thumbs 'round and 'round as he told us all how he came to this new country and how God has been good to him…that he has been blessed.

My Grandma and Grandpa Bettencourt.

Maybe that's where I get my interest in telling stories. His sincerity was so real.

My grandfather passed away at ninety-six years old. He lived a long and fulfilled life. I'm a better person because of him.

We all have those people who make a huge impact in our lives. My godmother, Jackie, would also be one of those people. She never forgot a birthday, Christmas, or Easter. She never forgot me. Some of my best times as a child were when I stayed over at her house.

My godparents were also raising their three children on a dairy, so I felt right at home. They had two sons and one daughter. The boys were a couple years older than me, and their daughter was one year younger than me.

Raymond and Jackie were the best godparents I could have ever asked for. When I did get to go and stay at their house, Sunday morning church is what I remember most. They were faithful to their beliefs, and it showed in everything they did. They also brought me to the Giants baseball game in San Francisco. That was the best! My godmother was not only a Giant's fan but also a bowler. She was on a bowling league. She would take her daughter and me with her to the bowling alley, where I would learn how to bowl. I thought bowling was the coolest thing ever.

Baseball games and learning how to bowl are only a few things I would get to experience as her godchild. There are many other wonderful things I could sit and write about my godparents.

But it wasn't long ago that I sat across the table from my godmother—just the two of us, really, for the very first time. At that moment, looking into her eyes and her looking back in mine, I knew that God had given me this precious gift. I couldn't have asked for more.

As a young girl, I didn't quite understand the importance of people like her. I was just happy to get out of prison, so to speak, because if I was home, I had to work.

Work was a good thing. In my adult life, I've come to realize I've never been lazy or overweight. I attribute this to a daily dose of discipline my father handed out. No matter how harsh that discipline might have been, it worked for me in some areas of my life…and not so well in others. There was not a healthy balance of work and love.

When my Grandma Bloomer would come to visit—my mother's mom—there was a calm around the house. I loved when she came! She didn't come very often, but it was almost magical when she did. Grandma was one of the best things that ever happened to me.

She made me laugh. She never yelled at me. She always looked *at* me. She loved me, truly…as I did her.

My precious Grandma Bloomer and my beautiful Mom.

My grandmother was an alcoholic. Of course, I didn't know this at the time, being just a small child, but my father did, and he never treated her decently. He was rude to Grandma. I didn't like him for that.

As I grew up, I realized that she did have a drinking problem, but her drinking still never merited my father's behavior toward her. I felt bad that her life was a rough, hard road. We all travel on some kind of road, and hers was doubt and fear, same as mine, which led us to some form of addiction.

So many frightened children grow up in an unstable, unloving world. My message is to change this somehow.

I carried the rejection I felt on my back like a big weight. The weight turned into rebellion. The rebellion turned into an "I don't care" attitude. If they didn't care, I didn't care...or I tried very hard not to care. But my heart yearned for acceptance and love.

Don't we all have our own cross to carry? My cross was my addiction, just like Grandma.

Someone handed me a joint one day, and I took it. Anything must be better than how I was feeling. It felt good. I liked it. It took me away for a while, until I was back into the scared and confusing environment in which I lived.

Pot makes you think. There's no denying that your mind goes into deep areas where you wouldn't ordinarily go. So, I thought about a lot of things, because I smoked a lot of pot.

But what I thought about most was God—wondering if He loved me, even if I smoked pot. I wasn't hurting anyone, was I?

Life is as hard or simple as you want to make it. This is very ironic for me to say! That's because I've made my life very hard for many years, being as simple-minded as I am. I have always carried with me a light, carefree spirit. I've been someone who enjoys most things about everyone.

Relationships are what I have built my life around. I've never been concerned much for things. I am a caregiver, always making sure everyone around me is OK...except me.

My life on the dairy had molded an innocent child into a hard-working, frightened, and confused but giving person. The more I gave, the more I thought someone might notice me. Sound like anyone you might know?

Don't we all grow into who we are, for the time spent with those around us? I do believe we do.

Like I mentioned earlier, we lived on a dairy. My father worked very hard—sunup to sundown. Milking and feeding the cows; overseeing the work that we, the girls, were doing; irrigating the crops for the animal feed; and always fixing something that needed to be fixed.

My father pretty much raised me, my sisters, and brother outside on the dairy—when we were old enough to venture out, that is. But Mom always had her hand on us when we were very small. I remember her telling me one time that having all of us so quickly together, everything seemed like a blur to her. I'm sure it wasn't easy.

The relationship with my dad at a young age was always filled with terror. You never knew what kind of mood he was in. So it was best to just keep your distance for fear of pissing him off somehow.

There were small bits and pieces of joy though. When we were small little girls, my sisters and I would line up to kiss Dad on the cheek before bedtime, if he was in a good mood. He would blow his cheeks up with air and when we kissed it, he would make it pop for us. I wish I could kiss that cheek today.

He would also give us rides in the scoop of the tractor. It was so fun, being so high off the ground. It felt like a ride at the fair. Mom was always so scared for us, but Dad knew what he was doing to keep us safe.

Christmas is another cherished memory—standing by the road anxiously waiting for Grandma Bloomer's arrival. How my mom and dad loved to decorate for the holidays! My Grandma Bettencourt and my mom's cooking was the best ever. Going to Grandpa Bettencourt's and watching him pass out the candy for everyone, as all the children were running wild with excitement.

There was this time when I was a very small child, I would sneak into our living room and turn on this electric wheel thing that went round and round with colors of blue, green, red, and orange. I would sit under our white-flocked Christmas tree and stare for hours as the tree turned different colors. Sometimes my sisters would join me—we wished we knew which presents were ours.

Shaking them and rearranging just so that they all looked perfect under the sparkling Christmas tree.

How I cherish the warm memories of yesteryears gone by!

But as I grew into a young woman, I realized that my father didn't have the skills it takes to raise *five little girls.* What young parent really does? It wasn't his fault.

Somehow, I felt sorry for him. I thought I knew more than him, because God had given me a noble and kind heart compared to the mean and angry heart that he had at the time. I felt like he was never really happy…until we all grew up and left. Then a *father* started to emerge. Someone you could talk to about anything.

I enjoyed my father much more when I finally grew up. He wasn't much for reaching out to us, but if you ever needed him, he was there—stable, like a rock. My father passed in 2004, and I miss our talks. I miss that rock. I miss my dad.

My mother has been a blessing to me from the very beginning. We don't really appreciate this person who brought us into the world until we experience the birth of our own children. Now I do. I don't remember much of my mom until I reached the age of twelve or thirteen. Before that, she seemed almost a blur. The reason was that she worked uptown and worked long hours, so I didn't see too much of her.

I remember babysitters and my dad always being there. The relationship with my mother never really got started until I moved out (or when she kicked me out when I was nineteen. I'm sure I deserved it. But that story comes later). All in all, my mom and I have open and honest communication. We respect each other's opinions even though we may not agree. I can truly say I'm glad she is my mother, and I honor her for all that she is. I love her more now than ever.

My oldest sister, Brenda, is a very friendly soul, but seemed distant as we were growing up. She was somewhat dishonest towards me in the early years. It seemed she took pleasure in watching me suffer. She liked to tell on me. But, apparently, that was her role as a big sister. I haven't had a close relationship with her in over twenty years. But our lives went in different directions. We have both hurt one another, but all is now forgiven. After Dad passed, I believe we've gotten closer. I see her a few times a year. And that's good enough for the both of us. But I always wished it were more.

Then comes my second sister, Balinda. We have always had a good relationship. The two of us have a strong bond. I believe we're on the same page, so to speak. It's a very easy, comfortable relationship. We didn't have to try; it was already there. She's simple, not complicated. She has a beautiful spirit about her, which I love to be around. She has made me laugh more times than any other sister ever did—and boy, as everyone knows, I love to laugh!

I'm the third oldest.

The three amigos. Benni, me, and Balinda.
My sisters are some of my best friends.

Then there's my fourth sister. She's beautiful, shy, timid, and meek, but yet very strong. Growing up, I was the caregiver to her and my youngest sister. I thought it was my duty to look after them, since no one else was.

We have always gotten along...except once. And that was my fault, and I hope never to repeat that mistake again. I hurt her. I told her at one point in our life that we had never been that close to one another—and that one comment ruined everything we had as sisters. It would never be the same again between us. I'm so very sorry I said that! It was dumb and immature. I never meant it. She doesn't give much of herself, just like my dad. If you want a relationship with her, you have to go get it. She won't offer. I pray somehow she knows how much I love her, even though our lives have taken different directions.

Bernadine—but we call her Benni—is the baby sister. She's friendly, outgoing, and easy to like and love. Most of all, she's honest and truthful. You know where you stand with her at all times. No guesswork is required. This little firecracker has always been there for me, and me for her. There is not much more I can say about her except, "Honey, you're best! I am so thankful that God made us sisters, but more than that He made us sisters in Christ. Peas and carrots, sister. Peas and carrots, always."

Last came the one and only baby boy. This little guy would follow me and my sisters all over the dairy. Growing up the only boy after five girls must have been hard for him. As I recall, we were very tough on him, but he was the youngest! So with that came a lot of teasing. He has always had a fun, lighthearted spirit about him. He's funny, outgoing, handsome like my father, and the life of the party. So easy to love, even though we have always stood our ground with one another. Together we would have some of the best conversations about God, and I loved he was so open to dialog with me. I believe we have always been close. We have had our ups and downs, but we loved each other enough to overcome anything that might stand in the way.

We don't get to pick our family, but if I could pick, I wouldn't change a thing. They're all beautiful people who have taught me how to love others unconditionally. I truly celebrate my earthly union with them. They have helped mold my character into the person I am today.

And that carries us to the title of this book. So who am I anyway?

Have you ever thought, *What would you believe about your Creator (God) if no one ever taught you what you know today?* Wouldn't you know or believe only what you've been taught? Now, take away religious teachings and figure it out for yourself.

That's exactly what I did. I couldn't believe that the Catholic faith or any one faith was the only right religion. I had too many questions. I started asking in prayer to God, "Who am I?"

Would this God I was being taught about really damn me to the fires of hell if I did anything wrong? Did this God love me? What was His definition of love? What was love? I was confused. I started on a spiritual journey way back around the age of twelve or so.

As I prayed to God every day, I would ask Him, "Who am I anyway? Why am I here?" The answers would come. For God is faithful to those who earnestly seek Him.

"I tell you the truth, my Father will give you whatever you ask in my name. Until now you have not asked for anything in my name. Ask and you will receive, and your joy will be complete" (John 16:23-24 NIV).

Chapter 2

Miracles Do Happen

The answers came. One by one and day by day, God showed me how to get through this life. My understanding at the time was to be quiet, do what you're told, stay out of the way, and get your work done.

One of my daily chores was also feeding the cows hay every day. After giving the calves their nourishment for the day, I would start my hunt for the wire cutters and hay hooks. Those were the tools you needed for getting this next job done. And for some reason, they were never in the same place that you put them. If you didn't have these tools on hand, you were like a fish out of water.

Sometimes I couldn't find the wire cutters and I had to use the hay hooks to cut the wire off the bales. You might ask, "Well, how would you do that?" It wasn't easy. But the job had to get done. The cows knew you were coming. You'd take one hay hook and twist it around the wire until the wire popped from the pressure it was under. The process was much slower. Wire cutters were a luxury.

Being outside on a dairy every day was amazing to me. I always would take the time to look up—up into the sky where all the birds of the air were. I would watch them fly and wished it were me. I wished to fly away to the land of milk and honey. To be free.

In some of my dreams I would fly. How I would just take off, right from the ground, flap my arms—and away I would go! I had the most adventurous flying dreams ever!

I've seen magnificent displays of every different sky possible—deep blues, the most awesome purples, and oranges, corals, and pinks that were just breathtaking. I've seen all different kinds of clouds too—strange shapes and sizes. It was so beautiful.

I had also seen many dark, crazy storms. And on this one peculiar day, it was no different—or so I thought.

As I made my way out to the feed the cows, the rain had just begun. I started throwing the hay in. The rain was coming hard and fast. I kept my head down and just continued. I was about halfway down the mangers…when suddenly the rain stopped. I looked up to the sky and saw the sun coming through the clouds. The sun's rays seemed to be focused right where I was standing. It was the most brilliant light I had ever seen, but for some reason it didn't hurt my eyes. And then I heard something. It sounded like a voice coming from the sky. What was it? Was I hearing things?

"You are special. You are Mine." I didn't understand where it was coming from.

But I was brave enough to speak back. "I'm not special. Nobody thinks I'm special. They don't even talk to me. They just tell me what to do."

The voice came again and louder this time. "You are special. You are Mine." I didn't know what to do. I just started to cry. The cows were all staring at me. I just stared back into their faces and started throwing the hay in again.

I'm not crazy, am I? Someone thinks I'm special? I'm going to have to give this some deep thought.

Voices from the sky? My first thought was God was trying to tell me something, but I didn't know He talked to people like that. Especially me.

I guess He wanted me to understand that even if you feel that your family, who is supposed to love you, doesn't (at least not the way you understand it), He does.

From that moment, I knew I had something important to do—God's work. Maybe it's to be more loving to the people who surround me. I wasn't quite sure. But I knew I walked away from that day a changed individual.

I didn't tell anyone what had happened—not in detail anyway. I didn't want anyone to think I was crazy.

When I finished feeding, I walked into the house. My mother was home cooking dinner—something I didn't see on a regular basis. She was usually at work. My sisters or I would usually prepare dinner. But she was home that day, and I was glad.

When I saw her face, I was comforted. I told her I was special, but no more than that. She responded by telling me, of course I was. I don't know why she told me that—she truly didn't treat me like I was. You know that feeling, when people talk to you but never look at you while they're speaking—like you're not important. That is how I felt. But now I had a glimpse of someone making me feel valued. I couldn't see Him, though. But that's OK. I could feel Him.

That's where my journey began—a twelve year old knowing there's more to life than what's just in front of her—a spiritual knowing somehow.

As I would feed the cows every day, I took delight in watching the cows eat. As they ate, I would sing to them the songs that I learned from the sisters in religious instructions. "*Sons of God, hear His holy Word. Gather round the table of the Lord. Eat His body. Drink His blood. And we'll sing a song of love. Hallelu, hallelu, hallelu, hallelu-*

jah. Brothers, sisters, we are one. And our lives have just begun. In the kingdom we are one. We will live forever. Sons of God, hear His holy Word. Gather 'round...." The cows just loved it. They would all gather round to hear me sing. It was fun, and it felt good doing it for them.

My dog, Pokie, also came with me on my daily trails. She was a Manchester Chihuahua, with dark chestnut brown hair and gold eyebrows. She was a little overweight for her size but a great companion.

I was in the seventh grade when one of my best friends had a litter of puppies to give away. I asked my parents if I could have one. And to my surprise, it was a go. I was so excited! She would follow me wherever I would go. She loved me, and I loved her. It was a beautiful relationship.

One day, as I was feeding the cows their hay, Pokie wandered off without me noticing. I started calling to her. But she didn't come.

Maybe she was running after the ducks, up by the lagoon. She did that quite often. A lagoon is the name we give a big hole in the ground that pipes over the waste from the cow corrals. Think about a lake of poop, pee, and water all mixed together. I know, it's gross, but that's what it is.

The top of this lagoon has a hard, thin crust that covers most of it. So, if you touched the top of the crust it would move. Very scary area to be around.

I went up on the bank of the lagoon and started yelling for her. By this time I started to fear the worst—that she had sunk under all the crap. I felt sick. "Dear Lord, please help me."

Suddenly, I spotted her. She was at least twenty feet out, on top of the hard thin crust, and part of the crust was giving way. She was struggling to stay on top. "What do I do, dear Lord? I can't watch this. I have to get her...." And that's what I did.

Without thinking a second longer, with no one around, I walked out on top of the crust that wasn't holding up a ten-pound little dog, but held a ninety-pound, frightened child. You tell me what that was, if it wasn't a miracle. I picked her up gently and walked back to the bank of the lagoon. I looked back over what I had just done and knew it was a miracle. The crust was waving back and forth. God had held me up! I just knew it.

Pokie was a young girl at that time. She grew to be a beautiful old lady and one of my best friends. Pokie, I'd do it again, in a heartbeat, if I knew you were in trouble. There are a lot of dangers on a dairy, so you have to be smarter than the danger or have God as your friend.

You would have to figure things out on a daily basis, just to survive. I wasn't very smart the day I walked out on top of the lagoon to get my dog. But at the time, I didn't care. I wasn't about to lose something that I loved so much. I believe God saw my heart and knew before I was even born that I would bring comfort to those around me. He would use me in a way to soften angry environments. God had a plan. But growing up into a teenager kept getting in the way. That's only because I didn't know yet what I needed to know.

Timing—everything is timing.

God's timing.

I was not the popular kid in school. Not the cheerleader or the most athletic. I wanted to be. But it wasn't possible with my daily home life. I had to work. There wasn't time for much fun.

I had a group of some really cool friends. Friends that if I called them today, we could sit and reminisce about all the fun we had in school.

My motto became, "If it's not fun, I'm not doing it." School was my escape. I was pretty good at it, too. I didn't have to try to get good grades. They just came. And it wasn't a struggle to have friends. They just came, too. And it was no struggle to get on the best side of my teachers.

I knew what I wanted and moved in the direction to get it. It seems almost like "noble manipulation." Maybe that's not the right description. But it's something like this: knowing how to get what you want, in the kindest way possible, as you allow the other party to get what they want, too. It was tricky at times, but I was good at it. I wanted to make others feel good. It seemed like almost my job or something.

This body my spirit wears longs to release the emotions that are so tightly wrapped in it.

Have you ever heard the saying, "It's written all over my sleeves"? That's me. I wanted people to like me. I tried to bring out the best in everyone—especially the boy who kept catching my eye every day in school. Here I am, at the end of my eighth grade year, almost a young lady...but not. I'm leaning up against a pole waiting for the bell to ring for my history class when I spot a boy. He was a few years older than me.

Back then, the seventh and eighth graders were mixed with the high school. Good thing. He was walking hand in hand with another girl who I definitely thought was not good-looking enough for him. I noticed his walk—quick, with short steps. I noticed how his butt looked in his pants; how his shirts were perfectly ironed; how his hair was just so. His mother must really look after him! He was so clean looking—so groomed. That's the man for me!

I fell. I fell head over heels in love with this boy, who didn't even know my name. He would probably never look at me. The girl he was with was all grown up. She had nice clothes and was the same age as him, which was sixteen. I was only thirteen.

I watched him for months walk to his English class with her by his side, as I waited for my history class to begin.

I told all my friends that I was going to marry him some day, have his children, and live happily ever after. "Oh, sure, Bobbett. You live in a fantasy land. He doesn't even know you exist."

One day I got up enough courage when he wasn't with his girl-friend, and I said hello to him. He said "hello" back to me. Now he knew my face. But I knew he thought I was too young. I was just a little girl who hadn't gone through puberty yet. He was a junior. But, I was going to be a freshman and him a senior. What was in store for me my freshman year? Another miracle perhaps? Someone to love me?

"Believe me when I say that I am in the Father and the Father is in me; or at least believe on the evidence of the miracles themselves" (John 14:11 NIV).

Chapter 3

First and Only Love

When it came to love, I believe I made it one of my highest priorities—to find the right man for me. I started noticing boys way back in kindergarten. My first encounter was with a boy named Patrick. I don't know if Patrick liked me, but I liked him. So I chased him every day in the school yard. He would always run from me. Thank God he ran; I don't know what I would have done if I had caught him!

In the second grade, I started to figure out what to do with them once I caught them. My first kiss was with a boy named Dean. My best friend Cheryl and I (always will be, even to this day!) asked him very politely if he would mind giving us a kiss. He didn't mind at all. So the three of us walked ourselves behind the school rooms so no one would know what we were up to. Dean stood in the middle and before I knew it, POW, right in the kisser. It was wet and mushy. And I thought to myself, *Is that it? This is what I was dreaming about all along? How disappointing.* He wasn't the one.

It wasn't until the fourth grade that I actually had a real boyfriend. His name was Freddie. He was so cute. He had blond hair and blue eyes. I was in heaven. We would hold hands on the way to the cafeteria. We would write love letters and pass them in class. There was no kissing in this relationship, just hand-holding.

Freddie and I went together for almost three years. It was at the end of my sixth grade year that he broke up with me. I was devastated. But I'm sure it was because we were going on to bigger and better things, considering we were entering the seventh grade. (Or maybe it's because of those stop-sign glasses my mother made me wear....) I don't know what it was, but I think I was still pretty cute.

Yes, I got glasses in the fifth grade, finally. Remember when I was a little girl and couldn't see? My world was a blur and out of focus from birth. This might be one of the main reasons I was so scared. Nothing was clear for me. I could not see! I was as blind as a bat. This made it extremely difficult for me—especially seeing the chalkboard at school or just trying to understand stuff.

I did not like wearing those glasses. But I could finally see.
6th grade, age 11.

I loved to read and write. My fourth grade teacher told me I had a gift for writing, so every chance I got, my nose was in a book. I love books—the feel of a book in your hands or the smell of the paper on which the words are written. I even love the thought that people took their time to write down all their stories, just for you and me to read.

I must say, books are my passion. If I could describe my heaven, it would be to be able to read every good book that has ever been written and all the time in the world to read them.

The summer entering the seventh grade would be a year that I would try to forget. My sisters and I would go to the Hilmar community pool almost daily. This is where I got my first kiss—French kiss that is. You know…tongues. I don't know if I was ready for that, but it came anyway.

The story goes like this. It was a hot summer day, and I'm sure my sisters and I had to beg for a ride to cool ourselves in the pool that is located in town, a couple miles from our home.

My dad was always busy or too tired to take us to the pool, so we had to bribe him. We would ask if there was anything we could do. He would end up giving us chores to do before he would take us to the pool—hoeing pie melons in the cornfield or pulling Bermuda grass in the most unlikely places (places that didn't matter, as far as I could see). But, that was my father—always trying to teach us something. Just, I never knew what....

This particular day, a young man by the name of Adam wanted my attention. He dove off the high dive and fancied his way over in my direction. He sat himself down at the end of my towel and asked me ever so politely if I would like to take a walk. I accepted his invitation. The high school sits right next to the pool.

So, he decides to take a walk over in that direction. We end up inside the gymnasium. It smells musty, like old wood. It's dark, and my skin feels cold. He then grabs me, pulls me in like I'm Scarlet O'Hara, and plants a tongue action kiss on me that I'm not prepared for. I pull myself away and tell him I thought we better go back. We do.

I learned a valuable lesson that day: Never be alone with anyone you don't know. I had a few boyfriends over the next couple years—no one important. But nothing was ever going to prepare me for this next boy. I watched him daily as he walked to his seventh period English class.

It was at the end of my eighth grade year when I spotted him—this young man I was going to marry. Somehow, I just knew he was the one! At the end of my eighth grade year, I got brave and told one of his friends that I liked him. His response was, "No way! She's way too young!"

That's OK. I'll wait. I knew how to get what I wanted.

The year I met Marlin, 1972, age 14.

I started dreaming about a life with Marlin the summer of 1972—Marlin James Bettencourt was his name—the same last name that I had, but no relation. You know when you know something and you don't really know how you know, but you just do? That's how I felt with Marlin. I *knew* I was going to marry him, have his children, and live happily ever after.

How did I know? I made it happen, with God's guidance, of course. Nothing is done without Him involved—just like the flowers and trees. They don't try to grow, they just do. So it is with life. Go with it, knowing that God has blessed you with the ability of understanding true grace.

I'm so grateful to be a part of God's great plan and having the awareness as I go. Do you see the simplicity in that? What you give is what you get.

If you believe with all your heart and mind that you are doing something good for the glory of God, Creator of heaven and earth, He will give it to you. He loves you that much. I know God loves me. Finally, I know this. He has shown me more times than I can count.

Over the summer…I became a woman and my body changed in a twinkling of an eye. Marlin's eyes were looking over in my direction now! Where once stood a small child now stood a petite four feet, eleven inches (and three-quarters) young woman of 105 pounds—almost a perfect figure eight.

He wasn't the only one looking my way!

I walked on to the high school campus confident, tightly wrapped in a pink body suit and purple suede hip-hugger bell-bottoms. I looked hot.

I had four or five guys ask me to the dance, which was coming up. One of them was Marlin. Guess who I picked?

My dream was coming true! This must be heaven. Someone, for the first time, was looking at me. Someone older, even!

Someone respected me.

I went home that day from school totally exhilarated with the expectations of love—real love. For the first time, someone else, besides my family, had a chance or choice to love me. Showing love to someone was all I ever wanted to do. Marlin made me feel important.

That night at the welcome dance was everything it could have been. We danced and talked together. He was really nice—so different than the other boys. The first kiss was after the dance, while sitting in his car. I had never felt something so tender.

I had my first real kiss in Marlin's 1972 Mach 1.

I wasn't loved on much or touched. So this was all new for me, and it felt good. Life just became exciting. Feeding calves was almost a joy—especially if Marlin came to visit me as I was feeding them.

I was only fourteen. I couldn't date yet. So he would sneak over and see me. It was fun and exciting all at the same time.

God gave me an excuse to get up in the morning and feel good about it. I couldn't wait to see Marlin at school every day.

I was in love.

Marlin drove a brand-new 1972 Ford Mach One. It was mustard yellow with black stripes down the sides, mag wheels, and flaming pipes, jacked up in the back like a cat in heat. It was a cool ride. But, of course, I couldn't ride in it. My dad would have killed me.

I have to mention again the first time I sat with him in his car at the welcome dance. I'll never forget. It was so clean and smelled brand new. It's the first time he kissed me. I still think of it as my first real kiss. His lips were soft. He smelled so good.

He was the one. I was elated! It was a happy time full of excitement. My sadness was gone.

Marlin gave me his class ring to wear a few weeks later. I wore it proudly. We were in love.

I know I was young, but I wasn't too young to know how good it felt to be loved. By the end of my sophomore year, we had become intimate. I knew what I was doing. Marlin never forced himself on me, not once. I wanted him. It's true. I wanted him. I hand picked him.

But what was handed me next was something that hurt me down to the core, and the scars would linger in and out of my life because of one sad choice. These next words will be some of the hardest words that I write. But they need to be said.

You know how we can stick things away in the dark corners of our mind and sometimes pretend they don't exist? But you know they do. Until this day, Marlin and I have only spoke about what I'm about to write a few times. And then, only recently. We were young, irresponsible kids…having a great time enjoying each other's company—maybe too much.

But not knowing too much at the time, I ended up getting pregnant. *I'm almost sixteen years old, and I'm pregnant.* What do I do? Do I have the baby? Before I knew it, the decision was out of my hands. Marlin had told his older sister. Within a few days, Marlin and I were on our way to a hospital in San Francisco.

I was to have an abortion.

We pull up in front of the hospital. I open the car door to get out. I turn to Marlin and ask him, "Are we sure this is what we want to do?" He nodded yes. "OK." Tears welled up in my eyes as I walk up the steps into the hospital.

I would never be the same. I was killing our baby. This precious little rose, this tiny fragile flower was never going to get to bloom. *Is God ever going to forgive me for this?*

The ride home was long and painful—physically, mentally, and emotionally. It was over, but the wound remained. Marlin and I went on like nothing happened. But the pain was deep.

I will never forget you, little one.

We did take responsibility to protect ourselves so that wouldn't happen again. I went to family planning. There I received birth control pills. We were safe to love again. But where was I to keep these pills so no one could find them? I needed a secret hiding place. I took a knife and cut a small hole in the side of my mattress. No one would find them there.

Or so I thought….

I had been taking the pill for a few months. Everything seemed to be going my way, until the day I reached in to get my pills...and they weren't there.

And all of a sudden, someone was paying attention to what I was doing.

Oh, *now* they care!

Who was it? Who found them?

I called Marlin to tell him about the missing pills. His voice sounded scared over the phone.

"Bobbett, you're not supposed to be calling me."

"What do you mean, Marlin?"

"Haven't you talked to your parents?"

"No."

"Your mother called me and told me to stay away from you or your dad was going to have me arrested for statutory rape."

"What?"

"Bobbett, I'm sorry. I love you, but I have to go."

I hung up the phone. Dumbfounded.

I went to my room and cried uncontrollably.

I'm sure someone was going to be showing up soon, acting like they care or something like it. Another grand display of how dysfunctional this family is. But I guess all families have their own dysfunction going in their home.

To me my parents were angry people; or they were just in a bad mood most of the time. Angry about what, I don't have a clue. Maybe their life didn't turn out the way they had wished it would go. Or, maybe it was about having sex. Not that they ever told me anything about it.

I want to know who told! Who found my pills?

Later that night, my mother comes in my room and proceeds to tell me I wasn't to see Marlin anymore. I find out it was one of my older sisters...like I didn't know that. I knew she was relishing in this one. I hated her for that.

She was about to get married. All the sisters were to be in her wedding. I didn't want to be a part of it. But my parents made me.

I was sixteen years old and felt like my world was falling apart.

I lost my virginity.

I lost my baby.

I lost my love.

Now, back to a family who say they love me but don't act like it. Perfect. I poured myself into my friends, and they were glad to have me back, so to speak, but weren't happy about the situation. They all knew how I loved Marlin.

It seemed like everyone in school knew what happened. I felt ashamed. I wanted to run and hide.

I found a "good" hiding place.

Marijuana. Beans. Speed. Black beauties. Christmas trees. You name it. It was 1975. Drugs were everywhere.

Marlin was just starting a new farming business, and I was starting an addiction.

And we weren't together. And it gets worse—I found out he started seeing his old flame again. Perfect.

I prayed, "Dear God, what do I do?" I remember what God told me a long time ago.

It is what you say it is. Hold all your positive thoughts toward Marlin. If it's meant to be, you'll be together.

One of Marlin's first tractors.

I held that thought. We would be together one day soon. It was tough over the next year, but I made it.

We had been apart for almost a year. It was the end of my junior year when we spotted each other at a high school football game. I hadn't seen him in so long!

He looked so good. He came over to talk to me. We had so much to say, but all I wanted to do was kiss him. I missed him fiercely. We went for a ride and talked about what we were going to do.

Marlin had decided to go talk to my mother. He waited for her to get off work. As she was walking to her car, he approached her. "May I have a word with you?" he asked. My mom was surprised. My family had thought, especially my dad, that he just wanted a piece of me and got it.

"I love your daughter, and I want to marry her someday. How can I show you that I mean what I say?"

My mom responded by saying, "You just did. Let me talk to her father."

It took a lot of guts to do what Marlin did. I was so proud of him! Someone was sticking up for me; it seemed like the first time. He loved me!

The next thing I knew, Marlin came over to give me an engagement ring. It was the only way my father would agree that we could start seeing each other again.

I was so happy. I had my man back. What he didn't know—and I didn't myself, at the time—is how an addiction was about to invade our lives.

Why did this addiction have to find me?

"We know that the law is spiritual; but I am unspiritual, sold as a slave to sin. I do not understand what I do. For what I want to do I do not do, but what I hate I do. And if I do what I do not want to do, I agree that the law is good. As it is, it is no longer I myself who do it, but it is sin living in me. For I know that good itself does not dwell in me, that is, in my sinful nature. For I have the desire to do what is good, but I cannot carry it out. For I do not do the good I want to do, but the evil I do not want to do—this I keep on doing. Now if I do what I do not want to do, it is no longer I who do it, but it is sin living in me that does it" (Romans 7:14-20 NIV).

—

Chapter 4

Growing Up an Addict

As I grew up, I watched my parents smoke—Lucky Strikes for my dad, True Blues for my mom.

It was something cool to do back in those days. They grew up in the fifties—the age of innocence before the fall. My grandmother on my mother's side also smoked—Pall Mall's, no filter. She was a tough old broad.

I guess it would only be logical to follow suit. Monkey see, monkey do. One copies the next and so on and so on. We are a pretty primitive species, though. Humans have only been here a second compared to the dinosaurs. The dinos got to stay for millions and millions of years. It doesn't look like that will be our fate. Power and greed says it all. God gave us a choice, and I believe a lot of humans have pretty much blown it.

We still haven't figured it out—how to get along. It's such a pity. Sometimes I think the best thing is a big asteroid to knock us off our block...total extinction in two seconds. Then you wouldn't have to worry about all the pettiness and ignorance of the world, because we wouldn't be here. Right? Remember, it's timing—God's timing. It was 1973, and the Vietnam War is what I remember most...boys coming home, broken in spirit, some with no limbs. Many never returned. Grieving and pain.

I remember picket signs. Lots and lots of picket signs. So many young people were angry at our government. I was angry, too. Peace, love, dope was the motto then. Make love not war.

That war did come to an end and, with that, our generation ushered in an age of peace and love…with dope. The war of drugs was on.

Some of the drugs were hard-core, and some of them weren't. I tried most of them but stayed away from hallucinogens like LSD or needles.

My first experience with anything that alters the mind was ciga-rettes. My sister Balinda was already smoking when she introduced them to me. There was a ditch that ran along the side of our house. It went for a mile or so. When they weren't irrigating, my sisters and I would go exploring in the ditches. We knew it was a safe place. We believed we were far enough away.

We sit face-to-face—Indian style. I'm fourteen. She's fifteen.

She smoked Marlboro reds. They're a tough brand.

She hands me a cigarette.

I took it.

Bad choice #1.

She tells me to light it. I take a puff and cough a little. She suggests sucking a little harder. I do. I start to cough like my head is going to pop off my neck. Everything is spinning. I was dizzy.

But I think I liked it. Figures. I take another drag. Cough some more. But I continue. We got up and started back. I feel like a grown-up.

I never told Marlin that I had started to smoke. I hid it from him. I didn't want something like that to ruin what we had.

It was like I was almost two different people. I was this prim and proper young lady for Marlin, and then on the other side I was a wild, carefree spirit with my siblings and friends—daring and eager to have fun and enjoy life.

Marlin was pretty much all about work. But he did make time for the important stuff. When I wasn't with Marlin, whom I absolutely adored, I was partying with my friends and trying desperately to balance it all—family, work, Marlin, school, and friends…and drugs.

I'm sure my parents did the best they could with the skills and knowledge they had. But at that time I thought their parenting needed some work, because I absolutely did not want to spend my time around them. I believed they were lost lambs, just as me.

Smoking pot on an everyday basis was something I looked forward to. It would take my mind and ease it. I was just copying the adults before me; I just chose a different substance. (Not my parents though, they were not drinkers, only socially.) Some individuals drank alcohol, and I smoked pot. Yes, pot is illegal. But, alcohol was, too, at a time. So I decided…if I had to pick the lesser of two evils, to feel comfortable in my own skin, I picked pot.

I had experienced enough to know the difference between alcohol and pot. I didn't like the way alcohol made people act—nor the way it made you feel the next morning, or that it made you pee too much. All in all, I picked what seems a less harsh way to experience being high.

Some of my best times were hanging out with my friends. Doing nothing but sitting around smoking pot and talking about God. We would ask each other, "Does God still love us, even if we smoke pot? Does a God exist? What do you think we're doing here on this planet?" We would have these heavy conversations—deep conversations, and I loved it. It was really the first time other people had paid that much attention to some of the things that were sensitive to me. Was this marijuana going to wake up a sleeping people—this loving but angry generation? So what happened?

A generation of people ended up plagued with substance abuse just to cope with all the insanity it had to offer. Just to cope. The music—just listen to our music of the sixties and seventies. We were trying desperately to tell a story. But no one listened.

We've grown from those confused kids into a loving, compassionate generation. My generation went on a quest for a higher power—searching, always searching for truth.

Is there any to be had? We had to find out. Something bigger than ourselves was needed to save us from ourselves. What happened to a loving people? What happened to caring about our planet? What happened to trust and respect?

I believe a time is soon coming that every knee shall bend and every head shall bow in the presence of our Lord. Because…it's not about me. And it's not about you. It has always been and always will be—because there is nothing else—but God, our merciful Lord and Savior, our Creator. Abba, Father.

The One who gives life. And the One who takes it away. He's our atonement. Our Redeemer and our Salvation. I didn't understand all of this at the time. I was too young and naïve. I just wanted to take the pain away, and I was very successful for a time.

My first encounter with drugs was when I was a freshman. There were a group of kids I knew that smoked pot. Their laid-back, not-a-care-in-the-world attitude was their trademark. They all hung out at The Trees, a place the students named for the potheads. If you were hanging with the kids who hung at The Trees, you were labeled as one of them. I was curious as to what they were doing to get that attitude. It looked kind of cool. No worries, so to speak. I needed to find out. A few friends of mine and I walked ourselves out to The Trees. The aroma was enticing and was something I had never smelled before. Somewhat inviting.

I was already smoking cigarettes. So what's the big deal? What's a little pot going to do to me?

Bad choice #2.

I take a hit.

It tastes dry.

Take another hit.

I start to feel a light buzzing in my head. Not overpowering though. Just a light, carefree spirit. Wow. This is cool. I feel my spirit—my soul.

What is this stuff? I like this feeling.

From that one moment in time, my whole life would be shaped. I didn't know it, but I had an addictive personality. My life became about how I could get high without anyone noticing. High is where I wanted to be. So the next few years, it was all about how I could get drugs and stay high.

Now, I had to be tricky. Pulling this off wasn't going to be easy. It was going to take some finesse. I was very sneaky, though. The only problem was the smell and the red eyes. I had to cover every base. I had a bottle of Visine in one pocket and perfume in the other.

Oh, and a Snickers just in case of the munchies. What are munchies? "Munchies" is a term that originated in the sixties or seventies for the hunger you felt after you smoked some weed. For some reason, weed makes you hungry. So, for everything I did, I was covering up—hiding cigarettes, hiding birth control, hiding drugs, hiding sneaky behavior. Hiding dead calves. Remember the calves? They didn't go away.

And most of all, hiding my feelings. Hide, hide, and more hide. I felt ashamed of who I was. What was I hiding from?

I don't know. No one was asking—or listening.

As my addiction started to grow into something bigger, my mind and flesh were always looking for the next fix. I knew it was wrong. But I figured, if my parents didn't have time for me, how in the world did God have time for one small, insignificant being such as myself. I was a pothead. I hid this best from Marlin.

Marlin had no connection at all with drugs or alcohol. He was a hard-working, clean-cut young Portuguese man. I admired him for his endurance and stamina. How I loved him so.

As each day came and went, my addiction grew with it. It was my last year in high school. Being a senior is supposed to be one of your most memorable years and it most definitely was. I was high

My senior picture I gave to Marlin, 1976, age 17.

What I wrote to Marlin on the back of the picture.

all the way through, but graduated—I really didn't have a problem in getting things done, and one of those things was my homework.

My parents had been having some problems. Problems I hadn't been aware of. The day my mother told us that she was leaving my father, I thought the ground had just dropped from underneath my feet. I was so angry. What did she mean?

Leave? A separation?

This isn't good. It's my senior year. I'm totally think-

Senior Prom, 1976.

ing of me and not them. I wonder what their problems were… They didn't really fight. Not in front of us anyway. Maybe she had enough mental abuse. I was still angry she was leaving us, though. Before I knew what was happening, my mother had left.

Oh no, this is not happening.

She was gone.

I hated her for that. My father was torn. I had never witnessed him in such a weak and vulnerable state. I hadn't seen his tears before. It was heart wrenching. What was my mother doing? What had my father done to her? She just left us kids home with him, this sad, angry man.

But something happened—something that was very unfamiliar. My father started to talk to us. A relationship with my father? That was something I never had before—didn't know if I even wanted it.

But something made me feel sorry for him—his tears. Had he had enough? Was he tired of being the bully?

I saw a more gentle side—one I could live with. I didn't need her to come home after what she's put him through. But I didn't know her side. Not yet anyway. I'm sure she had one.

Standing back and watching all of this play out made me realize that he was more than just my father, he was also a person who hurt...but desperately tried to hide it with his anger.

She was gone for a few months and came back at the end of my senior year. I guess my dad had to beg her to come home. So when she came, she kinda had a chip on her shoulder. She was not the same, and neither was my father. And neither were the ones left home, who endured it all.

I didn't want to speak to her. So, I was quiet. I knew if I opened my mouth, nothing good was going to come out. So, I stayed quiet.

I graduated. Barely. Not that I didn't have what it took; I just didn't apply myself. I didn't care. And it seemed no one else did either.

Getting stoned just seemed simpler. I got to erase things away. I was tired of thinking about them anyway. I was almost nineteen years old. It was time to start my own life.

A year had almost gone by since Mom came home. I was still feeding calves and pressure washing the barn each morning before they would start milking.

Then one day I had enough! It was time for me to make an exit—to leave. I was a cocky little shit who thought she knew more than her parents. My mother didn't know what was coming. Neither did I.

I was doing some laundry and trying to mind my own business when she said something to me that I didn't like very much. I turned to her and called her a f—king bitch.

Never before had I talked to her like that. I believe I had no more respect. At that moment, all she could say was, "Get out. You get out now."

I looked her square in the eyes and said, "Gladly. I'm out of here."

I went in my bedroom. I started to pack and asked one of my younger sisters if she would like to move out with me. She did. We left our youngest sister and little brother home. I would have loved to have taken them too. I felt bad, but I had to go. I loved my brother and sister. But my sister and I were on a roll.

We found an apartment. We found jobs, working for Valley Fresh, pulling cooked chickens apart. The money was good, but the job sucked. It was only temporary, though. We were young adults living on our own without a clue. But we had each other. We would be OK.

Sharing an apartment together was short-lived because Marlin and I decided to move in together. We found an apartment in Turlock—Rivera Apartments on Pioneer. It was a two-story building. We lived on the second floor above the managers. They were great people to have as landlords.

It was fun to start a life with Marlin. Now I would be able to see him every night! In all my nineteen years of life, which wasn't much, all I ever wanted was for someone to look at me and tell me that they loved me. My dream was coming true. My dream was to marry Marlin and have his children.

Marlin was everything. In the next few months, we decided to get married. I called the Sacred Heart church to make an appointment to come in and talk to the priest. The Father of the parish answered.

"Hello."

"Hello, Father. I'm calling to make an appointment to be married in your parish."

In his Portuguese accent, he says, "You need to find a boy-friend first."

Confused, I ask, "What?"

"You need a boyfriend first."

Sharply, but nicely, I say, "Father, I need to make an appoint-ment to get married in your church."

"You don't sound old enough to have a boyfriend."

"I'm almost twenty, and I am serious."

"NO! You need a boyfriend first."

"You've got to be kidding me."

"No, you need a boyfriend first."

I hung up the phone and just stared. What was that? The priest must have had too much wine! I was never so blown away in all my life.

By this time, my mother and I had mended. Family events brought us to speaking terms, but not close. My Grandma Bloomer, my mom's mother, was sick. She had cancer.

My Grandma Bloomer danced in and out of my life as a child. If I added all the days that I spent with her, they wouldn't add up to much. But I cherished every moment.

The memories of my grandmother are some of my best.

Teaching my sisters and me how to do the twist while listening to Elvis Presley. Doing your bouffant hair-do with the stickiest hair spray ever invented, Aquanet. She would stand in the bathroom with only her bra and girdle on and tell me stories about her life. A fifty-cent piece and sometimes a silver dollar would be her gift to us girls every time she came to visit. She made us homemade rolls. I can smell that fresh bread baking now. Her love was all over them, and I knew it.

I loved her for loving me. My grandmother was my friend.

My mother told me a true story about when I was born. My Grandma Bloomer was married to a military man. His name was Richard Bloomer. He wasn't my mom's real father. My mother never knew her real father. When my grandmother was a young woman, she was mischievous, to say the least. She was pregnant at fourteen and had my mother when she was fifteen. Grandma was somewhat of a wild bird, growing up in the back woods of Arkansas.

When I was born, she had just gotten back from Spain. Grandpa Bloomer had been stationed there. I was the new baby when they came home and became the favorite. It stuck with her. When she looked at me, she *looked* at mc. She gave off energy that I was attracted to. It was real. I knew she loved me. It was a love I wanted all the time.

I didn't care that she was an alcoholic. I loved her deeply. So when my mother called to let me know Grandma had cancer, I put my sword down. I wasn't fighting anymore.

My mother and I were talking, and I told her what had taken place on the phone with the priest. She couldn't believe it either.

I figured I didn't need the Catholic church. I don't believe in half the stuff they believe in anyway. I started making arrangements to be married in Lake Tahoe, Nevada. The date was set for August 25.

My Grandma Bloomer took a turn for the worse, right before our wedding. She passed away on August 21. We were to leave on the 24th for Tahoe. I felt so bad for my mom, for she was the only child.

After Marlin and I were married, which was wonderful, we had to come home and bury my grandmother. There was no time before.

Our wedding day, Lake Tahoe, 1979.

She was a shining star in my eyes. She dazzled me. It was a sad time to see her go. She had lived a hard life. I knew my grandmother was at peace now.

At twenty-one years old, I was married to the man of my dreams and covering my pain with drugs as my grandmother did with alcohol.

I was a fish hooked on a line. It seemed like my lifeline at the time... Always struggling. Always fighting to get free. But I was hooked.

What was next? It was only the two of us now. Or so I thought. Three months later, I was pregnant. Baby makes three.

"Trust in the Lord with all your heart and lean not on your own understanding; in all your ways acknowledge him, and he will make your paths straight" (Proverbs 3:5-6 NIV).

Chapter 5

My Boys

I had quit pulling greasy cooked chicken apart for a living and found a better job uptown, a nice family-owned business: Walter's Camera Shop. It was a nice place to work until my pregnancy got the best of me. The owner couldn't handle my mood swings, so they let me go.

I probably wasn't the nicest person, as I remember it. Not that the pregnancy was giving me problems, but being pregnant and not having a great relationship with the one I just married is what I was having trouble with. Our marriage started out a little rocky, to say the least. We weren't getting along very well at all. I was thinking maybe this was a mistake. Maybe we shouldn't have gotten married.

But, like I said, three months into our marriage, I was pregnant. I was using protection, but it didn't work. Marlin wasn't too happy about having this baby. I believed he thought I did it on purpose, but I didn't. It had gotten to the point that we weren't even speaking anymore. I figured I'd give him his space and me, too. He wasn't talking to me anyway, and when he did, it was a no-care attitude. I thought it was time to leave.

After only six months of marriage, I left. My parents had a mobile home that sat across the road from theirs. I stayed there until the end of my pregnancy. It was a very confusing time. I was twenty-one years old. I had lost my job, lost my man, lost my marriage.

But I did have this baby to think about. This little person growing inside of me. What kind of mother would I be? So young and immature. I wanted to be the best mother ever.

I knew I didn't have the right tools upstairs to get the job done right. I hadn't been the most responsible person. I stopped doing drugs while I was pregnant, but I was still an addict. I just didn't know how badly yet.

I needed to learn, so I read all the books I could on parenting. Everything I read wasn't anything like how I remembered being raised. I knew I wasn't going to raise my voice in anger. I knew I wasn't going to hit my children. I knew I would never reject them, belittle them, and ignore their cries.

I would look in their eyes and see the people they were.

I knew there was a little person in there that just wanted to be loved. I vowed to love this baby with all my heart, mind, and soul.

All summer long I floated in my parent's pool. There wasn't anything else to do. I had a beautiful tan—so much that my OB doctor decided to make a comment about how nice my tan was while my feet were up in stirrups. Now that's a nice picture. Nine months pregnant, as dark as a chocolate Easter bunny, and he's making a comment about my nice tan! How lovely. It takes all kinds.

My due date was August 15. Marlin and I had decided after being separated for six months it was time to come back together as a couple—to try again.

I packed up the few things I had and moved back to our apartment. I was elated to say the least. I had never wanted to leave. But we did need some time to think about what was ahead of us. A new baby on the way. No money to speak of. A small apartment. One black Chevy pickup. And a new farming business. We didn't have much but each other and time.

When I moved back to the apartment, there was nothing to do but wait for the baby to come. Marlin worked sunup to sundown. I made sure everything was perfect for him—dinner on the table when he came through the door, a spotless house, myself looking as nice as I could, being big and pregnant (I never liked being pregnant).

One day, as I was on my way to the laundry room on the backside of our apartments, I met a young woman. She was lying on a chaise lounge relaxing in the sun. She asked when I was due. I responded by telling her, "Now!"

She introduced herself as Julie. She and her husband were from Michigan. He had been stationed at Castle Airport Base. They also had a six-month-old son by the name of Jeremy.

God had sent me a new friend. Right when I needed someone, that someone showed up. We have remained good friends to this day. We spent the next couple weeks getting to know each other. It was nice. She was also a nurse. She helped me a lot through this time. I had many questions, and she was so eager to answer them.

The next two weeks came and left, and still no baby. I was now two weeks overdue.

My friend Julie and her son Jeremy from Michigan, 1980.

My doctor's appointment was August 28. When the doctor took one look at me and said, "This baby is ready to be born. For a little lady as yourself, you may have an eight-pound baby in there. Let's get you admitted to the hospital and help move this along."

I was so ready. I was admitted to Emanuel Hospital at around 11:00 a.m. that morning. I called my sister Benni. She was my Lamaze coach. She got there, and I felt better.

Nurses started sticking things everywhere—fetal monitors in two places. As they were placing an IV, Marlin showed up. I was glad he was there.

We watched the medicine drip in the tube that was supposed to induce my labor. I was scared. By mid afternoon, I had started having contractions. By late afternoon, they were coming hard, but I wasn't dilating. I was only at one centimeter.

The contractions were coming harder and faster but I wasn't dilating. By now it's almost 9:00 p.m., and I was tired. The doctor came in and said, "We have to take this baby." It was too much stress on him. I signed the consent forms, and off I went to the OR.

I'm awake during the procedure. They give me a spinal. I can't feel the lower half of my body. It's strange.

A nurse holds my hand.

I hear, "Knife."

I close my eyes. I pray to God my baby is going to be OK. I start to cry. It's all so overwhelming.

Then I hear a scream.

The nurse looks me in the eyes and says, "It's a big healthy boy!" They lay him on my chest for just a few seconds. He's perfect! Before I know it, they whisk him away as I start to go under.

It's been quite a day…

I woke up in the recovery room. My mind moved back to my new baby boy. He was so little and red. I couldn't wait to see him again. Marlin and I had made something together! It's the most magnificent thing I had ever experienced.

It was early in the morning when they finally brought him to me. He was tightly wrapped in a blue blanket. They had placed a cap on his head. I wanted to see all of him. I gently took his cap off. His head was shaped like a cone. The nurses explained to me that when a baby stays in the birth canal too long, that is the result, but assured me it would round out.

He was beautiful.

He was a very calm little boy. Olive skin. All ten digits. So tiny. Only a mother can appreciate this first look. It's quite a miracle.

God certainly knew what He was doing when He put this union together. I believe this was part of my heaven. It had to be. It by far outweighs anything I've ever experienced. The most precious encounter yet to this day.

Marlin arrived at the hospital the next morning with flowers in his hand. I did love this man so. One of the first things he asked was, "What are we going to name him?" I knew I wanted something that represented strength and love. It didn't take long for us to decide.

Michael David Bettencourt.

Michael means "beloved" in biblical terms. Then there's the archangel, Michael. And how about King David? I knew his name would serve him well.

C-section moms get a couple more days to rest and heal. I enjoyed the attention, too. My nurses were the best. I was home in a few days. Marlin and I were also doing a little better. Our new baby had somehow pulled us back together.

Michael. Our little Michael. He was like an angel. One day the two of us found ourselves together, looking over this beautiful creation God has given to us. As we looked at each other and back down at this infant child, we knew we had to fight for this baby to have the most loving parents any child could ever ask for. I knew, through thick and thin, I would endure this test of our marriage. To hold on to what I knew to be true. I had been with Marlin for almost eight years but only married for a little over a year.

When Marlin and I started our life together, one of the things hanging over our heads was the fact that we did not communicate very well. We loved each other, that was for sure. You couldn't deny the passion we had for one another. But I didn't believe we were *friends*.

We had become lovers. We both wanted someone to love. Our relationship struggled for many years because of this. No real communication, just passion. Or maybe our passion *was* our communication. I didn't know. I just kept going with what was in front of me.

And what was in front of me? A strong and prideful man. One who didn't put much energy into people, only work. I understood that, for I watched my father do the same thing for many years. I guess it's somewhat true then—daughters do marry their fathers.

I am not taking anything away from Marlin or my father; they simply didn't know anything else but working. This is how they were raised. They both started working on their father's dairies at a very early age.

When I met Marlin, he was milking cows with his brother, while their father worked at another dairy close by to where they lived.

Marlin and his brother are fraternal twins, and as they grew up together naturally you would think that the twins would be close to one another. But no. Not these two twins. Marlin has told me many stories—as far back as he can remember, he never got along with his twin brother. They never had anything in common but their blood.

And Manuel, their father, never spent any quality time with his kids. No bedtime stories, no hugs, no time for school projects, and most of all, no communication.

So where was Marlin supposed to learn how to communicate?

When Marlin and I were dating, his three older siblings had already moved out. So it was just the twin boys living home with their parents. And their parents, Manuel and Vicky…what a pair they were together. Manuel never liked me. I don't know if I ever had an intelligent conversation with him before he passed on, and I was always at their home. Now Vicky, on the other hand, always had something to say, and she said it.

She was the one who made everything perfect for her twin boys. Three meals a day, clean clothes, and a home where you could eat off the floor if you wanted. She was the one who nurtured her boys the best she could.

I loved Vicky.

Now Vicky and I… What can I say about our relationship? Well, we were both very opinionated females and both spoke our mind. So at times, those two kinds of personali-

My in-laws, Manuel and Vicky Bettencourt.

ties would come toe-to-toe. But all in all, we did form a wonderful relationship, for she knew how much I loved her son.

And how did I love this man. I knew he was a man of few words when I married him. Very quiet and quite challenging. Yes, our relationship was one full of passion, but not one of understanding and respect.

I felt in my heart that I needed to show Marlin that all I ever wanted to do was to love him unconditionally, share his pain and joys, be the wife at his side, and be the mother of his children. I felt my very purpose for even being born was to help Marlin become all he could be as I showed him what true love really is all about.

He needed to be shown compassion and understanding. No one had taken the time to look him in the eyes and tell him how much he was loved or valued. God had given him to me, and I knew it. There was no letting go.

So a husband who didn't talk much and a new baby to take care of…why in the world was I still thinking of drugs when I had such a calling on my life?

Why couldn't I stop thinking about them? I shouldn't be thinking of drugs. My husband and new baby should be all I ever need… What was wrong with me? I must be sick.

It was getting close to Christmas, and I hadn't done any Christmas shopping yet. Marlin said he would watch Michael for a little bit. I was only gone for a couple of hours, but when I returned, the house was in disarray. Michael had gotten sick. Throwing up with diarrhea!

What happened? He was fine when I left.

I was up all night with him. He wouldn't stop crying. I called his doctor. He'd see him right away. Michael had what is called croup. It's something like the flu but much more serious. At four months old, this little guy was hit hard with high fever, nausea, diarrhea, ear infections, bronchitis, and congestion. He couldn't sleep, eat, or breathe.

Michael at four months in hospital, 1980.

He was admitted to the hospital. He was a very sick little boy!

His stay in the hospital was over *two weeks*. At one point, Marlin and I were thinking there may be a possibility we wouldn't be bringing Michael home… All this new mother could do was pray that our baby would get well. God did answer my prayers. Michael did get better, but never *well*. From here on out, until Michael was seven years old, my boy was sick with one thing or another.

But during it all, Michael was the best baby. He hardly ever cried. He just wanted to be loved.

He still has some remnants of a bad start in life—an ear so badly damaged by infections that a surgical procedure was needed to correct a hole in his eardrum. A cough that will never go away due to scarred bronchial tubes.

But my son never complained. He was, and still is, one of the best things that ever happened to me.

Our relationship will never be marred. The bond is too tight. As he grew into a young man, this son is never embarrassed to give his mom or dad a hug and tell us how much he loves us.

I looked in his eyes from birth and found a beautiful soul…one who looked back at me…a soul who just wanted to show you how much he loved you.

God is great.

You would think with something this precious that the desire for something so far from pure would never be on my mind. But it was.

The next few years would only strengthen my addiction.

When Marlin and his twin brother were seniors in high school, his brother had got his girlfriend pregnant. They were married, and together they would have two sons.

She and I would become good friends for a time.

When I had Michael, their boys were ten and eight. I loved bringing Michael over to play with them. All three boys just loved it. And Michael's aunt loved him so much. She would look him in the eyes and see a loving soul also. I love her for that, and so did Michael. (Michael knew how to connect with people, even at a very young age.)

Our children and friendship were not the only things we had in common between the two of us. You guessed it. The big "D" word.

Drugs.

We smoked a little weed together, and that was cool…until I was introduced to cocaine. Before that I was only smoking a little pot.

We spent a lot of time together over the next few years…loving our children as we got high. I know that sounds awful. But, we did. It's one of those things that you only know what you know until you learn something different. We hadn't learned what that was yet, but we loved our children. No one can take that from us.

Cocaine and marijuana—these two substances would have their way with me for the next few years, until I found myself pregnant with our second child.

And my relationship with Marlin? Well, he worked all the time, and we barely spoke to one another, so I hid all my secrets from him.

It was hard to stop doing the drugs. At twenty-five, I realized I had a problem.

The pregnancy would keep me clean, sort of. I couldn't wait for it to be over.

I pray the ones reading this story right now will see the insanity here, because at the time I had not a clue to how sick in the head I was.

During my pregnancy, my oldest sister and I had become closer, or so I thought. She had just had a new baby also.

But the reason we were hanging out was not so much the babies—it was the drugs. The babies were only our cover. We would go visit each other with kids in hand. Pass drugs back and forth. Do drugs.

Not in front of them, but…They were around.

It's hard to bear the words of some of these things I write, but I did do those things. And I cannot ignore the truth.

You're thinking, *How could you?* I was hooked.

I only knew what I knew at the time, which wasn't much, but I needed to learn so much more about why this was all happening to me. I always asked God why. But my understanding of who God was at the time was far from the truth.

My dad was big on custom hot rods. In his lifetime he had built a few—beautiful cars. The cars were so nice—he would enter them into car shows up and down California. They'd been photographed professionally and have made their way into many hot rod magazines.

I was proud of him.

When setting up for one of these shows, you need some help. Marlin loves cars, so when asked to help, it was no problem. Sometimes I would go, but towards the end of my pregnancy I didn't.

My oldest sister would sometimes also go. I believe at one of these car shows, Marlin and my sister were talking about my personal past. She decided at that time to ignore the fact that I was pregnant and her sister and tell Marlin something that he did not need to know about me. It happened while we weren't together, and I didn't even tell my sister this. She heard it secondhand. Not from me.

I believe she was jealous of me and seized an opportunity to set out to destroy what Marlin and I were trying to build. When Marlin got back from that car show, he wouldn't even look at me. He wouldn't talk to me. I didn't know what was wrong.

I still had two months to go before the baby was here, and I endured enough tears during that time to last forever.

Marlin never told me why he was mad. My sister still came over with her son to visit. She would come and console me about Marlin and me having problems. I told her everything. I trusted her. She stabbed me in the back…and turned the knife…big time. I wouldn't know the truth of what took place until after the birth of our second child, many years later.

Our second son was scheduled to enter this world on Friday, May 13. Knowing that I would be having another C-section was nerve-racking, but I was grateful that I wouldn't have to go through any labor pains.

I had another spinal with this baby also, so I was awake during the procedure. I remember when he was born…there was no cry. I got literally sick and threw up.

I heard in the background, "He's not breathing."

Marlin with his boys.

Next thing I knew, I woke up in the recovery room. No one was around. I shouted out, "What about my baby?" A nurse appears. She told me they had him on a breathing machine but he would be OK.

My first thought was that I hurt my baby.

I was so glad I made the decision to have my tubes tied at this time…so my ignorance wouldn't be able to run rampant in me any longer.

I started to cry as reality set in. I didn't deserve to even be a mother. What was I doing? I'd made some bad choices. I told myself I would never do drugs again. This baby would be the start of a new beginning.

But wait, there was someone else to consider—my husband, Marlin. Did he want a life with me? He still wasn't speaking to me, up until the day I was ready to come home from the hospital.

He loaded the car with the flowers and balloons and all my belongings. With our new little son in my arms, the first thing out of Marlin's mouth in months to me as he got in the car was, "I want a divorce."

I asked, "Why?"

"You know why."

Maybe I did. I didn't want to argue or fight over something I couldn't change.

I cried all the way home.

We named our new son Mitchell James Bettencourt. He certainly was a cute and adorable baby. Dark skin with big brown eyes.

The episode in the hospital with his breathing was frightening. The umbilical cord had wrapped around his neck. But thank God, he was OK.

When we got home, I pretty much just stayed to myself, taking care of my boys. Marlin didn't leave, and neither did I. We stayed together.

It was rough at times, but our marriage went through a refining process—get rid of the stuff that is causing you problems, and keep what you love.

We both kept what we loved—each other.

Now, wouldn't you think that with two beautiful sons and a reconciling marriage I would no longer even think about drugs, right?

Wrong.

This disease is so cunning and so baffling. This is why I sometimes questioned whether I'm sane or not. I had no control.

What is control? Isn't everything a control? Isn't it you or someone or something telling you when, where, why, and how much?

From 1983 to 1989 I was very lost. Through those years I never stopped searching for God's guidance. I would ask God "Why me?" and "Please help me. I can't help myself anymore."

At this time in my life, I allowed myself to become very heavily involved with the drugs. I was then doing a gram of cocaine a day.

But really, what brought me down to my knees was the *crank.* Meth. It makes you go fast. Too fast.

When I think of the drugs I used to do, it makes my toes curl up and sends shivers down my spine. There were so many times I thought I was going to die.

But I didn't.

I remember lining up the next line of crank and asking God to please help me as I continued in my indulgence. God must have saved me to do something for Him. I just didn't understand why I would knowingly hurt everyone around me if God was going to use me.

It's the only thing that makes sense to me now.

My son Mitchell was, and is, quite a joy. A few sniffles along the way and a bad temper at times were all the heartache this little fellow would ever give to me. Mitchell was a wonderful baby—and as cute as a button. It was hard to resist this little charmer for all the beauty that was wrapped in his face.

My son had a sharp wit about him. I noticed he had quite a curious mind. He liked to figure things out. His ability to understand common sense was developed, it seemed, at a very early age.

Every toy truck, or anything with wheels, he had to take apart and try as he might to put back together again. As soon as he figured out how to operate a screwdriver,

Trip to Yosemite, 1985.

all Marlin's screwdrivers were missing. I would find them every-where except where they belonged. I also would find hidden toys that he couldn't put back together. I'd just laugh, because I knew I had a clever little man on my hands, and I was proud.

No matter what, I took care of my boys. You would naturally question that. Because it doesn't make sense that if you can't take care of yourself, how do you take care of children?

I don't know. I must be an exception, because I gave all my time to my boys…except the few moments to do a line or two during the day. My boys were up early in the morning dressed and ready for the day. I had them on a schedule.

I made breakfast for them each morning—not just cereal but eggs and bacon and happy face pancakes. Everything was about having fun with them—play time with special projects.

Lunch time…where we made it together.

Nap time…where I would lay with them and watch them gently fall asleep.

Story time…where books came alive.

Snack time…where fruits and vegetables were wholesome, but chocolate was more fun to eat.

Dinner time…where the family comes together as one.

And bedtime…bedtime was the best. The three of us would come to know a nightly ritual, picking the book that I was to read to them. I loved to read to them.

I cherish the memory of two little boys, one at each side. They were so eager to hear how the book would come alive. Because Mom just didn't read it to hurry through, I played every character and played them well. Their favorite was *Green Eggs and Ham*. I love that memory.

I was the best Mom I could be. I was room mother at their school every opportunity I could get—always involved. And through it all, I looked at my kids and loved them more than anything.

But yes, I had a problem, and it was getting worse day by day.

The year was 1987. Marlin had become heavily involved in growing his new business, as he should be. I was alone from early in the morning till late at night, with no one to talk to and confide in. I felt like I constantly needed something to fill the hole.

This yearning was for a feeling of pleasure instead of the pain I felt. The drugs were a medication to cover all this pain and all this loneliness. I stayed in this frame of mind for nearly five years.

Over this time I would come to experience all sorts of characters coming and going out of my life. Some of these characters were good people who were just as messed up as I was. Some characters were godly people that the good Lord kept putting in front of me. But I wasn't paying attention. I was just going through the motions with no direction.

No willpower. No understanding of God's true grace. Lost. So ever lost in a world of madness.

The addict's mind is always looking for the next fix. Whatever your addiction might be, it was all about the wanting. The getting. The preparation. And the doing.

And in this madness, you're able for a time to forget your pain.

But it's still all an illusion.

The pain is still there, just covered up for a time. Our minds haven't reached a mature way of finding solutions to the problems that we have, without being exposed.

I was getting close to a big fall.

There were drugs in every direction I looked, except in the direction of Marlin. Thank God for his stability.

Marlin didn't know what to do with me. He just thought I was a bad person with a bad problem, and he didn't have the maturity level either to handle this situation well. He was mad at me most of the time.

I don't blame him. He was working every day to grow his business, and I wasn't helping. I was hindering.

This next stretch of time would send me spiraling down into my darkest hole yet. This is where I hit bottom.

It was 1988 or so, and my brother-in-law came to work for us in our harvesting business. So did a young woman, whom I will not name.

One day my brother-in-law showed up at my doorstep to tell me that he thought Marlin and this young woman were having an affair. He had seen them getting out of a corn truck together in the early morning hours. He thought it strange to be out in the field for no apparent reason other than...mischief.

He believed it was his place to tell me, him being my brother-in-law and all, that I was being cheated on.

I didn't know what to think or do. Something like that had never even crossed my mind.

What does that kind of information do to a person such as me? A lost soul.

Indulgence, that's what. Anything to take the pain away.

I didn't know what to believe after I questioned Marlin. He got mad and told me it wasn't true. But my mixed up, drug-infested mind wasn't able to filter this information well.

Could it be true?

With her?

Didn't seem like his style. Maybe I didn't know my husband at all. I know he didn't know me.

Why does it seem like everyone is trying to hurt me?

I wondered if my brother-in-law and sister were trying to hurt me. If so, they succeeded. It didn't make any sense.

My life was spinning out of control. I did more drugs to help the pain. But the pain would not go away this time. The bottom fell out from underneath my feet.

I was falling. Everything I ever understood vanished. I couldn't see anymore.

I hit hard.

A bottoming out is a horrible experience. You believe you are a worthless piece of crap and there is no way out. I thought about suicide a lot but didn't have the heart to do that to my kids. Michael was nine and Mitchell was six. By my own actions, I probably deserved every last painful thing that ever happened to me.

I couldn't leave... I had no money, no self-esteem, no value... The only good thing I ever did was bring my children into the world.

But I wasn't a good wife. I wasn't a good mother. I was *nothing*.

My addiction at its worst.
Christmas, 1988.

I stood at a crossroad...

I called Marlin at work and told him I was leaving him and the boys. My mind was fried. I didn't have any more control. The drugs had taken over.

I left my husband and my children.

"Do not be deceived: God cannot be mocked. A man reaps what he sows. Whoever sows to please their flesh, from the flesh will reap destruction; whoever sows to please the Spirit, from the Spirit will reap eternal life" (Galatians 6:7-8 NIV).

Chapter 6

Rehab

I called a friend of ours and asked him if I could stay at a home he had, which was vacant at the time. He allowed me that privilege. I didn't deserve it, but he was my friend, and a friend who didn't use drugs. Thank God for him.

The first night by myself was one of doing drugs until they ran out. I remember it so well. I cried at every line I did. I slept most of the next day, recovering from the all night binge. When I had straightened myself out enough to drive, I got in my car and drove back to our house. No one was home, so I went in.

I had remembered that I had hid some drugs in a drawer in Mitchell's room. I had to get it out of there. I didn't want the boys to find it and hurt themselves in any way.

I was coming out of Mitchell's room with stash in hand when I heard the garage door going up. I was busted.

Marlin was so angry at me for being there that he came at me, grabbed me, and pushed me out the front door. I was so humiliated. He told me to never come back.

What have I done?

I'd allowed drugs to ruin my family. I must be sick.

I went back to my friend's house and bawled my eyes out as I pleaded for God's mercy. I emptied the bag of dope I had down the toilet. I was done.

It's late, but I call Marlin. He answers. "Hello."

"Marlin, can I come back home?"

"NO!" He hangs up. I called back.

He answers, but doesn't say anything.

"Marlin, I know I have a problem. I need help."

"Call your parents."

"I can't. Please help me," I plead.

He still said no and hangs up. I call back.

"Please, Marlin. I'll call first thing in the morning and go to a drug program. I can't do this by myself."

Finally he says, "OK."

"Thank you," I sob.

Next thing I hear is a dial tone. I was so completely humiliated. But I didn't care. I just wanted to go home to a safe place. I got in my car and drove home. The garage door was up. I pulled in and shut the door. I was scared to go in. Everything was dark. I walked down the hall, turned to see my precious little boys fast asleep.

I walk over and kiss them both. I *had to* get well.

The morning came and the boys were overjoyed to see me. I was still their mom who has loved them for the last nine years with all my heart. I had changed every diaper, kissed every boo-boo, and wiped every tear. I missed them so.

I was so ready to go to a program. I knew I was defeated. I would miss the boys, but it was for my own good, and theirs, too.

When the boys and I woke that next morning, Marlin had already left for work. I started our morning like any other morning, but this time it would be with no drugs to get me through.

Out of some kind of obligation, I felt I needed to let my drug connections know that I wouldn't be back. I made a few calls, with no answers. I left a message that I wouldn't be back and that I was going into a drug treatment program. I'm glad they never answered; I knew they wouldn't. It was way too early in the morning for cranksters to be up.

I had one more source to tell. It was a family member who supplied me the most. Much for free. I needed to tell him face-to-face.

After I got the boys their breakfast, I start making phone calls to facilities around our area.

I found a place on the outskirts of Sacramento, up in the hills. The place was called Gull Haven.

I called my niece Tina and told her what had transpired over the last few days. I asked her if she would like to take a ride with me to check out this facility. My niece and I have always been close. She's like one of those rare jewels you like to have. I have one.

Tina has a beautiful spirit—so willing to give. I'm so blessed to have her in my life, as well as her family also.

Tina was eager to help, as always, so she went with me. I was scared, but knowing Tina was there, I felt better. Even though she is thirteen years my junior, she has the heart of a lion.

I love her so.

We made arrangements to make the two-hour drive the next morning. That gave me the afternoon to finish the deletion list of drug outlets. I got the boys off to school, cleaned the house to perfection, packed my suitcases, and prayed I would have enough strength not to use as I put myself in harm's way.

I got myself ready for the day, feeling the pull and urge to use all along.

It was going to be OK. I can do this.

I drove over to the family member's house who had supplied me. He thought I was there for the usual.

He hands me a bag of dope. I stared down at it and back up at him and, with tears in my eyes, I say, "No thanks, I'm done. I'm going to a treatment program in the morning. I needed to tell you in person I wouldn't be back, and after I get home from the program I can't have any connection with you at all. I'm sorry, but I can't do this anymore. I almost lost my husband and children because of this drug." He was already separated from his wife and kids because of his addiction.

He looks at me and says, "You'll be back."

"No, I won't," I whisper under my breath. "I don't want this kind of life. It is no life at all. It's madness."

Calm as a cucumber, he says, "Well, good luck. I hope it all works out for you." I give him a hug…and out the door I went with no drugs on my person. I was so proud of myself. I did it. Well, actually it was the little angels that would be home from school soon. I rushed back to be there when they arrived.

Evening came, and the house was still and silent when Marlin walked through the door. The fragrance of roast beef coming from the oven filled the air. The boys and I had just finished reading one of their favorites, *Green Eggs and Ham*. As I watched the boys jump from the couch and run to greet their daddy in their little feet pajamas, I realized again what I almost gave up.

Tina and I got an early start. The traffic was heavy as usual. But the drive went fast. We talked the whole way. I was excited to be on a new course.

A nightly ritual.

When we pulled into the driveway, it looked like a place that I would be able to appreciate. The facility sat on a few acres of rolling hills with big old trees in all directions. As I look past the trees, out into the field, I saw horses and cattle and chickens, too.

God knew what I needed—to come back to basics. There's nothing finer than nature at its best.

I loved it.

It was an old ranch style home—probably built in the forties. It stood with grandeur. For if its walls could speak, oh the stories they would tell.

We knocked. An older couple by the name of Chet and Audrey answered the door. Chet was a big burley man with passion written all over his face. Audrey, small and meek with her voice soft and inviting. They were the directors as well as the owners of Gull Haven. They had been expecting me.

I told them, "The place was great. I like what I see, and I'll be back tomorrow." They didn't want me to leave. They thought I might not be back. They'd seen it one too many times. But this time they'd be wrong.

We were at the peak of corn season. Marlin couldn't find anyone to help pack the pit for the length of time it took to take me, so my parents did the honor.

September 27, 1989, was the beginning of something new. Freedom.

I often wondered what they said to each other on that ride home. Would they blame themselves? Or would they blame me? Or was there a place to blame anyone?

The conclusion was yet to be seen.

But I am the one who did the drugs, the one who made all the wrong choices. I did take the blame—guilt-stricken blame. I had a lot of animosity built up inside of me and didn't know how to express it. The drugs seemed to wash it away—made it better for a time.

But now I was being faced with the truth—hard truth—which some people in my family might not want to hear.

The truth was, I was tired, and I was tired of it *all*. I needed to rest. My mind had been in full throttle for so long.

My parents pretty much dropped me off at the front door. This is what they needed to do.

Chet and Audrey met me at the car. I introduced my parents as Chet offered to help with the bags. They showed me my room and told me to get settled in. I would be in detox for the next three days, so they wanted me to get as much rest as possible.

I did. I slept and stayed to myself for the next few days.

As the drugs started to slowly come out of my system, I felt an overpowering feeling of relief. The pressure was gone to get high. The mind is a very powerful thing.

All kinds of feelings that the drugs didn't allow to surface were making themselves known. There was no holding back the torture that I felt.

I did not want to be what I had become. But there it was—sitting there, staring me in the face.

How could I redeem myself, dear Lord? I have broken almost every rule.

The first thing I needed to do was admit I'd become powerless over the drugs...to believe in something bigger than myself.

Well, I knew that.

But knowing it and *implementing* it are two entirely different things. I needed to totally understand this concept. It was somewhat foreign to me.

There was a bigger picture, and not just what was in front of me at that moment. This was all an illusion. A nightmare. I needed to wake up and start living in the now and present.

I shared a room with a woman by the name of Sally. We bonded almost instantly. I had quit smoking cigarettes years ago, but that first night in our room together, she offered me one, and I took it. Capri Menthol Lights—the skinniest cigarettes I had ever seen. It tasted sweet.

She needed a friend as badly as I did. We sat up that night and told each other our stories. Her story was heart wrenching. We cried and laughed and smoked. It was good. Sally was tall and lean with lots of wrinkles; her hair was thinning, her teeth rotten, sores on her face. It looked as though someone had recently beaten her black and blue. The bruises were obvious.

We were probably the same age, but she looked much older. I thought I had done lots of drugs until I met her. At the end of my drug abuse, I was snorting about a gram a day. She was shooting three. I never used a needle. I was too afraid.

Her family found her in an alley, passed out and bloody. They thought she was dead. She told me she prostituted herself for her drug habit. Her family gave her one more chance or that was it. They brought her here. She'd been here only a few days.

I thought I had a bad life until I heard about someone else's!

Our room was small and plain. Pictures of Jesus and posters with positive affirmations were arrayed on the walls, bringing it to life. Two twin beds were stuck in each corner with old blue blankets for the cover.

This would be my home for the next twenty-one days.

When detox was over, I was ready to come out to meet the rest of the group. In all, I believe there were about ten to twelve individuals in the program at the time—some young, some old. By the looks of them, some were worse than the others.

But, as we all know, it's hard to judge a book by its cover. Nobody knows what's inside until you look. I prayed this was what I needed.

Our room was right off the kitchen. The aroma of bacon and sausage filled the air. My nose followed the scent. There, standing in the kitchen and holding a spatula, was a tall, slender, good-looking black man. As he turned to greet me, he took my hand by the fingers, lifted it to his lips, and delicately gave it a kiss.

"Good morning, mademoiselle. How did you sleep?" He introduced himself as Armando. "Do you drink coffee?" he asked as he poured me a cup.

"Yes. Thank you," I answered.

He sipped his coffee from a small clear glass with no handle.

I asked, "Don't your fingers burn holding your coffee like that?"

"Just for a little while. This is the way all Frenchmen drink their coffee."

"I'm French, too. Only half though."

"What's the other half, my darling?"

"Portuguese," I proudly said.

"What a combo," he remarked, with the biggest smile on his face. "I'm the number one cook around here," he told me, "so please, no complaining."

"I won't. I don't eat much."

"Well, I'm here to fatten you up, little girl. And aren't you a pretty thing."

"I don't feel that pretty," I said.

"You don't worry about a thing. Armando will get some good food in your system, and you will be feeling and looking like a million bucks in no time."

I was taken by his charm. No one had taken that much time to notice me in years, and that conversation only took thirty seconds or so.

I came into the program probably weighing ninety pounds or less. Old scars and fresh sores told a story all over my face. I was ashamed of the way I looked.

It was hard to sit across the table from others and not feel embarrassed. I had always been kind of cute. I wasn't so cute now. I was hoping rest and good nutrition was what I needed to get my body and brain restored!

Breakfast was served. Armando had a bell he rang to draw everyone's attention. Pancakes and eggs, bacon and sausage—breakfast was quite a treat. Sitting across from people I didn't know wasn't that bad. We all were talking about our families and how this could have happened to us. It looked like a good group.

A few of us were young, one old, and the rest around my age. I wondered if there was a reason for that—a large percent being my age, that is. It didn't matter though—we all had a problem. We all needed help. I believed I was ready to dive into this program with flippers on.

The daily schedule was a routine of mealtime, chore time, and group time, followed by one-on-one time with the counselors. All the counselors and helpers were ex-drug addicts. They knew the mind that we were dealing with.

Their compassion was real—not fake. They really wanted us to grasp that there was a life outside of drugs.

I remember going for long walks. I found myself sitting out in the fields, staring into the sky. A large number of birds flew overhead. They were chirping loudly and making all kinds of noise. They had not a worry in the world. I longed for the freedom they had.

I've always had a connection with birds. Growing up on a dairy, you see all kinds. They fascinated me. I loved the idea that they could fly. Have you ever really examined a bird's feathers close up? The detail of how perfect and soft they are is amazing.

Now, it was *my* turn to learn how to fly.

Whenever I found a bird in trouble, like falling out of its tree, I would try to nurse it back to health. Most died, but I gave it my best shot. What fragile little things. I believe God gave us birds so we may understand the little and perfect things in life.

My understanding of this freedom was to surrender everything to God. To really be free was to "let go and let God."

A few times I went for walks with one of the counselors. It was part of the program to really get in there, dig deep, and find a root that was causing the insanity. She asked me one day what I thought might have led me to this point in my life. I knew.

It was *fear.*

I had been afraid all my life—afraid of not being loved, of not being wanted, of not being good enough, of the dark. I had a fear of dying and not understanding why I'm here, watching others die and wondering where they go after they passed.

My fear was as relentless as my addiction. I tried to stop so many times, telling myself I wouldn't use again—swearing to God that I wouldn't—then turning around and slapping Jesus in the face again with my insanity.

I feared just being *no good*—a bad seed, so to speak, which no one really wanted anyway.

I hid my fears all my life in a bubbly outgoing personality.

No one knew how this drug had trapped me. The drugs took this fear away, even though only temporarily.

The counselor explained insanity to me in words that made a lot of sense: doing the same thing over and over again and thinking you're going to get a different result.

I needed to lean not on my own understanding but to lean on God and stop torturing myself. The devil had had his fun with me, and now it was *over.* I would not be his footstool any more!

They gave me literature and books to read…which I loved. One was *Narcotics Anonymous (NA),* and another was *Alcohol Anonymous (AA).* I was not an alcoholic, but I read what it had to say—all good stuff.

I paid very close attention to everything they had to say. There was a way to stay clean and sober. For me, I chose the twelve-step program. I prayed and studied over these twelve steps to freedom diligently.

I admitted I was powerless over drugs…that my life had become unmanageable. I came to believe that a power greater than myself could restore my sanity. I made a decision to turn my will and my life over to the care of God as I understood Him. I made a searching and fearless moral inventory of myself. Admitted to God, to myself, and to another human being the exact nature of my wrongs and that I was entirely ready to have God remove all these defects of character.

I humbly asked Him to remove my shortcomings. I made a list of all persons I had harmed and became willing to make amends to them all. I made direct amends to such people, except when to do so would injure them or others. I continued to take personal inventory, and when I was wrong, promptly admitted it. I sought, through prayer and meditation, to improve my conscious contact with God as I understood Him, praying only for knowledge of His will for me and the power to carry that out.

Having had a spiritual awakening as the result of these steps, I tried to carry this message to drug users and to practice these principles in all my affairs.

These steps changed my life.

As I put these principles into practice, my knowledge of who I really am started to come into focus.

I was not put here on this earth to find, indulge, and get high every day. *My purpose was to love everyone unconditionally.* I made a vow to my God that I would do whatever it took to stay clean.

I walked into a drug treatment program, tired and defeated... ugly, inside and out. What walked out twenty-one days later was not the same person who walked in.

I was rested, clean, confident, and proud to say that, yes, drugs took me down, but I didn't have to *stay* there. I had a choice! I chose God, Marlin, and the boys.

There was no communication allowed for the first week with any friends or family members. So when the week ended, I was overjoyed to find that the following week I could receive visitors. Marlin came up to see me alone the first time. We spent the weekend getting to know each other all over again. We had a day pass. Guess what we did? You guessed it! We had missed each other terribly.

The next visit, he brought the boys. I missed them so much! It looked like they had grown a foot. As always, Michael's little face was one of concern—he was worried about his mom. My little guy, forever looking out for others. Mitchell's interest was more into the old red tractor he spied sitting out in the field—always the little farmer.

The four of us took a picnic lunch out to where that old red tractor sat and enjoyed the sun and just being a family again.

Everything is going to be all right, I thought to myself.

My parents came once to one of the meetings. It was family night, but I was still surprised they came!

But I picked up a vibe: They really didn't want to be there. My gut was right. When I did get home, they never got involved in learning or attending anything to do with my recovery. They were the ones who brought me into this world and raised me to believe you stand by

Rehabilitation Drug Center, 1989. Michael and Mitchell find a tractor to play with.

the ones you love. But they didn't want to know the harsh reality of why I was in this arena of life. Just like never really wanting to know me. Nothing changed, just the date for them. I loved them, but I wished it had been different.

My brother and his new wife came to visit also. He's the only one of my siblings who made an effort to be a part of my recovery. Possibly because the others were still involved with drugs at the time, as far as I knew.

And my new sister-in-law…I would come to know her as one of the people in my life that I could trust and be able to count on whenever I needed her. She's like one of my own sisters, even better. Their two little girls are both my godchildren. This couple is very special to me.

My sister Brenda, the one who I thought would be the last to send me a care package, did. It was in a brown paper box, which she had decorated with flowers and teddy bear stickers. Inside was a funny card of how she wished me well and some of my favorite candy. She knew I loved chocolate! It also had magazines and colorful pencils. I cried at the thought that she had thought of me.

One of our challenges in the program was to write a letter to someone who has hurt you to a degree that you believed reconciliation was not in the equation. Then never send it.

I wrote a letter to Brenda. I scribbled every bad thing I thought, that she ever tried to do to me. Then I needed to forgive her.

I would in time.

There were many things I learned in the twelve-step program and many things I learned from the ones I lived with for nearly a month. I thoroughly enjoyed being there. I enjoyed the company. The understanding of one another. I enjoyed learning about my addiction and what it can do to a person. I enjoyed learning that I do have value, no matter what others have to say about me. I enjoyed telling the truth. I enjoyed the food and mealtime. I enjoyed getting in touch with my Father in heaven.

I enjoyed being *me* again.

The day I went home was the day of the earthquake in San Francisco…October 17, 1989.

I will never forget that day as long as I live. One of my worst fears was to be somewhere else but home and not be able to make contact with my loved ones when something awful happened.

It was all happening as I dreaded!

The phone lines were not working. I wasn't able to get a hold of Marlin until later that evening. I told him I needed to be home. He got in the car and came to get me. He didn't arrive until after midnight.

On our way home, Marlin dedicated a song to me that was playing on the radio. "If I Could Turn Back Time" by Cher. Our lives were heading in a different direction. I was so excited to be me again.

It had been so long.

"But the fruit of the Spirit is love, joy, peace, forbearance, kindness, goodness, faithfulness, gentleness and self-control. Against such things there is no law" (Galatians 5:22-23 NIV).

Chapter 7

Friends

To be me again—it sounded so good. But, what did that mean? I didn't even know who I was. If I wasn't the drug addict, then who was I? A daughter, sister, wife, mother, and friend? Well, yes, this is true.

But I do believe I'm a child of God first…and then those other titles come into play. But I knew playing them would be a whole new game.

I understood to seek the kingdom first and then all will be given unto me. I believed in all that, but somehow I just couldn't quite implement it. Not at 100 percent anyway. Or even 50 percent for that matter.

I was out of rehab but had a long way to go in my recovery and my relationships, especially with my Holy Father in Heaven—I was just trying to remember it's one day at a time.

On our way home, Marlin let me know about the surprise he had waiting for me. Over the last twenty-one days, while I was gone, he had started to redecorate the house—new carpet and paint, new curtains and light fixtures. I couldn't wait to see what he had done for us!

When we arrived, the house was in total disarray. I didn't care. I was just so glad to be home.

Marlin wanted everything fresh and new. One of the things I failed to see, before I was clean, is how much this man loved me. I had been numb and blind for so many years.

I plunged into my recovery with zeal—attending NA meetings, connecting with a sponsor, reading and educating myself about this disease I have, and praying to God for healing—body, mind, and soul.

With different eyes, I saw my children for the very first time. How precious they were to me. One of my highest priorities was to reestablish my relationship with them. Looking at an eight and six year old and explaining the reasons why mommy had to go away for a while was difficult, but doable. I needed to prove they could trust me—that I would never leave them under those circumstances again.

But through my actions and the love I would give them day-to-day, they did. At this time, guilt and shame played a big part into this sad but joyous saga. I was going to beat this addiction, with the grace of God by my side.

Children are so resilient. They hold no judgments in their hearts. They just want to be loved. My boys never showed me any hostility or anger for my absence. They missed me, as I missed them. This was all that was important to them.

I got myself involved in the boys' school, which was difficult at first. Some mothers were very blatant about their feelings about whom or what they thought they knew. They treated me like I had an infectious disease, sometimes, saying hello only when they absolutely had to and sometimes downright ignoring me, like I wasn't even there.

Some parents' attitude suggested that they were better because they never needed or wanted to take a drug to begin with. And they wondered, how could I not be thinking of my children first? I never called this disease to me—not any more than my father called his diabetes to him or the cancer that took my grandmother. Yes, I have made some bad choices. But haven't we all?

These people didn't know that I never, ever believed I was first at anything. No one had ever put me first—my parents, my husband. I'm not feeling sorry for myself. That's just the way it was.

But, through a daily reminder, I've decided not to use drugs and, finally, *I had the confidence and courage to put me first.*

I believe the others who treated me badly were lost souls, as I was at a time, just in another way. Maybe blinded by their inflated egos or because their love for others didn't go very deep.

You can't catch being a drug addict. It's a choice to use drugs.

I know. Believe me, I know.

They didn't want me around them or their children. But didn't they know I went through a rehab—self-analysis on a day-to-day basis? And I did the best I could with what I had to work with.

Can't you be a little compassionate, I wondered. *Please?*

Sometimes I felt like I was in a dark, deep hole alone and my flesh was the only one who understood it—how I got here, that is… I was always trying to make others understand all of it. I knew they never would. You have to experience something like this firsthand to totally understand it.

My prayer was for their hearts to be open to love and compassion…that they wouldn't be blinded by ignorance or hate, that their judgment of others would somehow make them look at themselves and realize that we all fall and my fall was a public humiliation.

Trying to be pleasantly acceptable and not being received was painful, but I learned what God wanted from me: Love everyone unconditionally. Never judge one another. You just don't know what others have been through.

There are reasons for every lesson in life—reasons for every moment. And that one moment is all we will ever really have. Finding that reason is our purpose for being here.

This drug lesson? I'm glad I had it. It made me a better person.

I detached myself from them—the school mothers who shunned me. I accepted that they were never going to accept me, ex-drug addict that I was. I was labeled.

That's OK. God labeled me as one of His children long ago. So who were they to me anyway? A fleeting moment. That's it.

After a while, I kind of felt sorry for them. I started praying for their bad behavior to change so my boys wouldn't have to witness it. What is that Scripture? God gives you only what you can handle. So I handled it. I realized they only know what they knew until they learn something different. And as I was learning also, I prayed their heart would be open to mercy and compassion.

God had given me many tools to work with. One was grace.

I was eager to be of service for every opportunity that came available to help, whether it was volunteering in the classroom or being a room mother. I loved it. It gave me extra time to be with my boys and also the chance to enjoy the other children, too. Over the years the boys were involved in a lot of school activities and projects. I was there for everything. I never allowed other people's inabilities to stand in my way of progress.

I had a mission: To stay clean, to search for a better self, and stay close to God.

The boys wanted to play baseball, especially Michael. We signed both of them up to play. Michael was a pretty good ball player…and Mitchell, well, he couldn't hit the ball for anything. He always felt so bad that he couldn't hit it, and I also felt his defeat, as mothers do.

Come to find out, he couldn't see correctly. His perception was off. Where you would normally know when to swing the bat to hit the ball, he was swinging a few seconds after the ball had passed the plate. Something was definitely not coming together right. We sought professional help. Over time, his problem did correct itself. Mitchell would come to hit many balls. I was very proud of him.

I knew I had a light within me, but I didn't know quite how to make it shine—really brightly, that is.

My relationship with Marlin always seemed to move backwards instead of forward.

Remembering back what God had told me as a child, "You are special. You are Mine" I meditated on those words daily.

Life had beaten me down, but I was willing to face the world, the humility, the music…and fight back.

Because I'm a fighter, I knew I *will* win.

As I prayed to God to raise my thinking to a higher level than what I understood, an angel of mercy showed up at by front door. Literally. Her name was Ruth. She introduced herself as the pastor's wife of a Pentecostal church, not far from where I lived. I had only been clean maybe a few months when she graced me with her godly presence. As I opened the door, she instantly reached for my hand and told me that God had sent her here.

She had the look of an angel—a small frame, a tightly wrapped bun on the nape of her neck, a beautiful complexion, and a glow not from this earth. As she took my hand, I took hers and invited her in.

We instantly bonded. I told her that I had been praying for guidance to stay clean…and then she showed up.

Again, she explained to me that God told her to come to this particular house—that there was someone here who was hurting in a big way. She said the Holy Spirit led her here. I broke down into tears and told her it was me!

We were all on painful, unfamiliar ground. She led me to Christ right then. For the first time in my life, I had a friend who wanted nothing from me, except for me to know peace. And to know I had a friend in Jesus.

I wasn't quite ready to fall into the church scene but was ready for a one-on-one Bible study with her on a weekly basis. We started in the fourth Gospel, John. I had never even owned a Bible. I always asked for one at Christmas but never received one. We were Catholics. My parents thought I didn't *need* one.

If anyone needs a Bible, it's a Catholic who doesn't go to church! I fit the mold. I went out the next day and purchased one. It was the best purchase I ever made. Over the next few months Ruth and I became good friends. I trusted her. The trust I had in her led me into their church. I had never really attended a church on a regular basis. I knew that I needed a solid foundation, as did my boys. We started going almost every Sunday. The boys enjoyed it so—my children learning about their Savior was everything I wanted for them. The boys came to know Jesus as their friend and invited Him into their hearts and were baptized, as was I.

I invited my family to the baptism, but no one showed…not even Marlin.

The church people were warm, friendly, and inviting. Their worship was loud and intense. The whole experience was phenomenal. I continued to go.

A year had gone by in an awful hurry. It was October, 1990. Marlin and I had grown apart, instead of drawing closer to one another. I was busy with the boys and him busy with his business.

I had asked Marlin often to come to meetings with me so he could better understand this addiction, but he didn't. I asked if he would come to church, but he didn't. Maybe he went once, but it was so different than the Catholic church he never went back.

Over time we lost all communication. I suggested counseling, but that was something he wanted no part of.

I was dangling at the end of a rope, ready to fall again.

I prayed a lot. Wasn't God hearing me? Tell me, what's worse, being alone...or being alone in a relationship?

One year later I relapsed.

It was Halloween. I knew where I could get it. The same people a year ago were the same people today. I was scared, but I followed through, knowing all along how risky this was.

I achieved the unthinkable. Drugs were in my possession.

I did a line.

I hated it...instantly. It made me feel weird...jittery. I didn't want to feel like this again.

I knew it was a big mistake.

I threw the rest of it down the toilet. I needed to take control of my life. No one was going to tell me what to do and how to do it from this point on.

Not Marlin.

Not the devil.

Not anyone.

Marlin and I needed changes. And if it was a separation or divorce, so be it. Bring it on. I was ready to fight for what I believe in.

Dignity. And it didn't help when someone makes you feel like a piece of crap every day. I wanted out of this ridiculous relationship where no one was winning.

Corn season was almost over. I knew he would be coming home grumpy and tired. With dinner in the oven, waiting for his return home, the boys and I were making our way out when he arrived home. I probably would have gotten away with this relapse thing if I would have gotten out of there five minutes sooner. But I was busted as soon as he took one look at my face. There is a look that cannot be denied when doing crank. Marlin told me he was leaving and never coming back. I told him I was sorry. I knew it was a mistake. I promised I would never do it again—which I haven't to this present day.

He didn't believe me. I wouldn't have believed me either.

He left. I put the kids in the car and went out to trick or treat. Marlin never came home that night. Or the next night.

As far as we both knew, it was over.

The third night came, and finally he walked through the door. I told him very calmly that I was going to look for work and then I would leave. I also promised him for the second time that I would never do drugs again. I knew it was wrong, but I didn't know how to make this work without support from him. I was not strong. I was weak and vulnerable.

At this time in my life, I asked God to dress me with His whole suit of armor. For I knew the devil wanted me back, and I did not want to walk into his camp again. I threw myself into the Lord's Word and stayed there, not letting go of my Bible.

Ephesians 6:10-18 KJV is amazing:

Finally, my brethren, be strong in the Lord, and the power of his might. Put on the whole armor of God, that ye may be able to stand against the wiles of the devil. For we wrestle not against flesh and blood, but against principalities, against powers, against the rulers of the darkness of this world, against spiritual wicked-ness in high places. Wherefore take unto you the whole armor of God, that ye may be able to withstand in the evil day, and having done all, to stand.

Stand therefore, having your loins girt about the truth, and having on the breastplate of righteousness; And your feet shod with the preparation of the gospel of peace: Above all, taking the shield of faith, wherewith ye shall be able to quench all the fiery darts of the wicked. And take the helmet of salvation, and the sword of the Spirit, which is the word of God: Praying always with all prayer and supplication in the Spirit, and watching thereunto with all perseverance and supplication for all saints.

Everyone deserves a second chance…don't they? Because, chances are, you could change. I was going to change and become the woman I always wanted to be.

It didn't take me long to find a job. I knew bookkeeping like the back of my hand. I put the kids in day care and started working for a metal company in Turlock. I was in a professional office, doing professional work—and doing a good job. Everyone liked me.

Marlin and I were still together. I didn't leave. I wanted our marriage to work. I wanted to believe he did too.

I worked for this company for almost a year. It was the summer of 1991. The owner had always treated the office girls to an overnight getaway to Monterey. I wanted to go. Marlin, of course, did not want me to. See the control?

It was a big fight, but I stood my ground. I was an adult who was not going to hurt anybody. I was going, and that was final. My perception of life now was not stuck in that same old thinking. I was blossoming into a beautiful flower, and I was leaving his old way of thinking behind. If he didn't catch up, he was going to be left behind. Monterey was wonderful. The ocean is always a beautiful place to go to think. It had been a long time since I had been anywhere and had some fun. All the girls were great. I loved that God allowed our souls to meet—even if just for a brief moment. When I look at that time in my life, I realize I'm a better person for knowing all of them. They helped me through a tough time. I thank them for that.

Marlin was waiting at the door for me when I got home that evening. He was not in a good mood. The only thing I can say is for the first time in my life, I was not afraid. I told Marlin if we don't seek professional help to save our marriage, it was over. I was not going to live the rest of my life afraid of him and what he might think, say, or do. I was my own person and wished him nothing but peace and respect.

He finally knew it to be true that we both needed help to heal our wounds. Marriage is *work,* and anyone who says it isn't needs to have their head examined. Sorry, but too many people don't take their vows seriously. They don't believe in the sanctity of a holy bond. I do. I believe in marriage—where the two shall become one and care and nurture each other, never seeking to hurt or harm in any way, loving unconditionally. That is what I had to offer as a woman to a man.

I didn't look back. Jesus had me on a new road, and I knew it. Marlin and I sought the help we needed. I recommend marriage counseling for anyone who has big issues hanging over their heads.

If you think you have the answers to life's most difficult situations, then why don't you have a book or two or a degree hanging on the wall to prove it? Counselors have a job, and it's to help you see the areas in your life that need some mending in a loving way.

It was the best thing Marlin and I have ever done together as a married couple.

I stopped working for that other company and started working for *ours*. Marlin and I and the boys are a team. We are going to make it.

One day Marlin came home and asked me if I wanted to take a ride. "Sure," I say. We jump in his truck, down the road we go, and I ask, "Where are we going?" "You'll see."

"I'll see? Is this a surprise?"

I love surprises. One of my best joys in life has been receiving surprises from him. To me a surprise is someone thinking of you— and only you. There's a thought process that happens when wanting to surprise someone. You do it when you want to share a loving and teasing moment which you will remember forever—*together.*

I call that love.

It was a short ride. We pulled up in front of a new home that no one had ever lived in yet. "What are we doing here?" I asked.

"Do you like it?"

"Well, of course."

"Well, I think I would like to buy it. What do you think?" Surprise-surprise! My husband and surprises!

We bought our second home February, 1992. It was a great house. I loved it. I loved my husband to pieces. The boys were thrilled.

Things were good. And they kept going that way for us. The business was growing. We weren't struggling as hard to make ends meet. The boys were doing well in school. Everything was moving in a positive fashion. I loved life, and life loved me. Oh, we still had our ups and downs, but that's the merry-go-round of life.

There were no more drugs. It was becoming fruitful in every way.

One day I got a knock at the front door. I open it to greet a woman. She had fire red hair with lots of thick red freckles, a little on the heavy side, thick glasses, clogs, clothing you didn't see people wear out in public too often, and the fairest of skin I had ever seen. Her hair-do looked something like a bush on fire.

She's standing there with a clipboard in her hands and I'm wondering if someone sent me a singing telegram. It's not my birthday. I'm sorry. But it was a moment. This lady left a lasting impression.

She was not a singing telegram but a woman on a mission. She was looking for host families for exchange students. It sounded wonderful. I accepted right away.

She explained that there were about ten host families in the area and the students would be sixteen-year-old females from Japan. I was excited to be having another female in the house. Early August was her arrival date.

When the day came, I picked her up at a local church in town. Her name was Yumiko. Her name fit her to a tee—it means "meek"—in every way. She was a tiny little thing. Her hair was cut short and was as black as coal. When she said hello, she bowed. It was so sweet.

Yumiko, our exchange student from Japan.

We didn't know each other's language, but we had no problem communicating. I gave her a big hug, and off we went to her new home.

Yumiko was with us for a month, and in that month we had numerous outings—trips to Yosemite, Monterey, San Francisco. Going down to our local river, throwing a pole in the water, and catching fish was one of her highlights.

Her stay with us was one of complete joy. The day she had to go was heartbreaking and full of tears. We had found a way to break though the differences, the language barriers, and truly enjoy the time we had together.

My husband and I were simple farm people. We enjoyed the small things in life. Having her stay with us was a blessing. God knew what we needed, and He provided that need in Yumiko. Our family will never forget her.

Over the years, we've lost touch with each other. There are days I sit and wonder what she's up to. I pray that someday our lives may cross again. Maybe because of this book, they will.

The days after Yumiko left were sad and lonely. I had desperately needed a friend. I still wasn't able to hang out with my sisters, for some were still involved in the drug scene. I missed them, though. I hadn't gone anywhere to meet new people or friends. The school mothers still hadn't accepted me. There were the church people, who were good people, but nobody seemed to click with me.

At the time, we had our nephew working for us. His parents had recently divorced. This kid had always been special to Marlin and me. We were glad to have him be a part of our family.

He had been dating a young lady by the name of Shelbey. I had seen her at our shop a couple different times and casually said hi, but I did not know her.

One day, she shows up at my door unannounced with a twelve pack in her hand. "I hear you've been kind of sad, and I'm here to cheer you up," she says with a big smile on her face.

I asked, "How do you know that?"

"I went by the silage pit, and Marlin told me that you've been sad since your exchange student left and that you needed someone to cheer you up. So here I am." I told her to come in, that I wasn't much of a drinker, but the company sounded good. Shelbey and I became good friends over time. Not only was I blessed with her friendship, but I would come to know and love many others through her. Three of these young ladies totally stand out. Dana, Evelyn, and Cindy. I love them like my own.

Shelbey and I.

I looked forward to their visits, which were quite often. We would sit outside and smoke at a white plastic round table and talk about all our worries, foes, and fears, our loves and our lives. We talked about everything imaginable under the sun and the moonlight, till wee hours in the morning sometimes.

The boys were always around. They loved the idea Mom had new friends. It was exciting to them and me, too. Mitchell had a pair of roller blades back then, and I remember we used to time him to see how fast he could fetch a beer out of the refrigerator in the garage. It was a great time for all of us.

There were a lot of tears and laughter around that table. But most of all, God had given me true friends. Friends you could count on in any situation, good or bad. I never knew that until they came into my life. I was thirty-four at the time. Shelbey was fifteen years younger than me. But that didn't matter to us. We were friends, and it was good.

I've been told before that you are mentally the same age you are the day you stop doing drugs as when you started. So, actually, I was younger than the friends I had. I was mentally fifteen years old; they were nineteen. They nurtured me until I could catch up.

This time in my life was full of joy. And one of my biggest joys was our annual trip to Pismo Beach every Thanksgiving. We would

Michael and Mitchell loving Pismo Beach.

load up our 4-wheeler, bikes, and dune buggy and go play in the sand for a few days with our boys and lots of friends.

Shelbey, Dana, Evelyn, and Cindy would also be there. The boys would ride all day, and then as night approached we would build a huge campfire. We all sat around the fire in a circle talking and laughing about the day's events. As I watched my boys roast their marshmallows over the open fire, I marveled over their happy faces. They loved this trip and also looked forward to spending time with Mom and Dad.

Michael, Pismo Beach.

And especially riding their bikes! They would ride from sunup to sundown. They have been riding ever since they were four years old. They are both great riders. Start them young, so they learn respect for speed.

The other joy I would come to know was the friendship with Shelbey. You see, I never had a friend that didn't do drugs. Ever since high school, everyone that I hung with did some sort of drug. So having a friend like her was very precious to me.

My grandsons Mason and Marshall at Pismo Beach, 2010.
Second go-round.

One Sunday morning the two of us decided to go to church together, and after the service was over we would hang out at her parents' pool. But as we were leaving the church service, Marlin called and asked if I would go pick up some parts at the John Deere

Mitchell with his son Manuel at Pismo Beach.

dealership about twenty miles from our home. We were in corn season and he needed them right away.

For some reason I decided to use the back roads instead of the highway, and boy, would I learn what a mistake this would be for the rest of my life!

Since Shelbey was already with me, she decided to come along for the ride...we thought we soon would be basking in the summer's sun at her parents' pool.

But that didn't happen.

We started our short trip on this back country road, not far from our home. As we were approaching a blind intersection with a two-way stop, I had the right of way. There was another vehicle traveling at a top speed...that decided to run the stop sign.

He hit us broadside in the passenger side. The car flew through a railroad tie fence, and we came to a stop in a field on the other side of the road. A railroad tie came to rest up on the windshield as I looked over to Shelbey to see if she was OK. She was. Thank the Lord.

Surviving the accident.

We got out of the car to find the other driver was also OK. I know I was traveling around 55 miles an hour, and the other driver? Well, not so sure, but I knew the impact was *hard*.

I called Marlin and let him know what just happened, and he was there in what seems like a few minutes. He was very thankful we were not hurt but mad as a hornet at the driver who decided to run the stop sign.

Shelbey's Mom showed up and took us to the hospital just to make sure we were both OK. As the days went by, I was becoming more and more stiff, with lots of pain in my neck and lower back. Shelbey would also come to know pain over the years from that accident, but over all she would be all right. But she was young and resilient.

But I was not that resilient.

The next few years would be nothing but doctor visit after doctor visit…and medication to deal with the pain. My back was a mess.

As the years slipped by, the relationship between my nephew and Shelbey started to sour…and for good reason. He had become involved with drugs, and that is something Shelbey would not tolerate. Nor us either.

We both gave him plenty of chances before we ended up putting him into a drug rehab. The same place I went, actually.

Shelbey knew it was over even when he was in the treatment program. But she's such a fine person, she saw him through it all. When he returned home, they tried for a while to make it work, but it wasn't meant to be.

But what *was* meant to be was our friendship, because *that* never died. It is as strong today as it was then. I will never find a friend more endearing than Shelbey. She has the heart of a lion. I love her so.

Our nephew kept messing up, and finally Marlin had to put a stop to the insanity that we had allowed to come into our home. He told him to leave and not come back. But our nephew would dance in and out of our lives for years…till this day, in fact—always with the same problems.

I wish more than anything that I could take all the pain that people feel and roll it into a big ball and throw it to the wind and it would disappear forever, but that's not real. What's real is God.

"For God so loved the world that he gave his one and only Son, that whoever believes in him shall not perish but have eternal life" (John 3:16 NIV).

Chapter 8

New Adventure

Sometimes when you look back on your life, doesn't it feel like a dream? Or maybe even a nightmare? But you know it isn't, because you have all the proof that you lived it.

At the wonderful age of thirty-eight, it seemed like my life had really just *begun*. The fog was finally clearing, and I could see a brighter future.

The boys were both teenagers and following in their father's footsteps. I had friends that I never knew were possible. My family was coming back together. I had a marriage that finally felt like one. All the puzzle pieces were starting to fit.

The whole picture was coming to light for me, but for Marlin, there was one problem: a business that he didn't want at the time.

While going through the constant stress of a growing business, my husband was not happy with what he had created, meaning the harvesting business. During oat and corn season, I knew Marlin would be coming home tired and beat from a long day's work.

In a harvesting business, you have a very small window of opportunity to get the work done. It requires articulate planning. Each move must be thought out very carefully.

Our harvesting business, 2000.

I remember night after night Marlin coming home in a bad mood from his day's toil. There was always something wrong somewhere. But I do believe it is the nature of the beast. You have huge equipment, with all moving parts working to their limits, pushing to get to the next job site. Something has to give somewhere at some time. And a lot of the times, it was my husband who broke. I did my best to let him know that everything was going to be all right, but he was never satisfied with the status quo. He thought there must be an easier way to make a living than bowing down to clients who treated him like a second-class citizen as he threw himself out there to do the best job he could.

I can hear him now, like it was yesterday, "I'm selling this damn business. I'm not doing this next year. I'm selling out!"

I heard it year after year.

Softly as I could, I'd say, "If God takes care of the birds in the field, He'll take care of us, too." Or something like, "It is what you say it is." That was not what he wanted to hear—a spiritual concept. I knew what he needed, but he had to figure it out on his own. I couldn't do it for him.

Chopping corn, 2011.

I told him I loved him as God loves him and pretty much left it at that, night after night, year after year.

It was nice to see Marlin have one passion—NASCAR. My man loves the races. We have been to numerous races—Daytona once and Las Vegas for the last fifteen years. So when he wasn't working, I would find him in front of the television, rooting for his favorite driver, Dale Earnhardt Sr....and scribbling down different business opportunities for me to check out.

Marlin and I at Hoover Dam in Las Vegas, NV.

My man loving the races in Vegas, 2008.

I would catch him up in the wee hours of the morning, watching infomercials on buying foreclosures or anything that looked better than what he was doing.

We bought business opportunities he saw from TV that looked good but never panned out. But he kept searching. He wanted to buy a franchise. We looked into buying a Taco Bell, or an In and Out, and many more—to no avail.

Then one day a young man called Marlin and asked if he would be interested in looking at a business opportunity. Marlin knew him pretty well, so he said he would listen. He was curious as to what it was, so we had him come over, and he started to draw out a bunch of circles on a piece of paper.

It was a network structure where you start helping others and work your way up to financial success by teaching others to do the same, through selling products that you are already using; now you just get paid for doing so. They called this business Amway. We had heard of Amway before but never thought it was for us. It sounded good, so we decided to take in our first meeting to find out more. When we walked into the meeting place, the men were in suits and ties and women in dresses below the knees. At first we thought it might be a religious order of some sort.

Now, we are country folk, and I don't think my husband had ever owned a suit and tie. This was going to be something quite different.

Were we in for a wild ride! So we rode this thing called Amway, and we rode it hard. We were excited at the possibility that we could find financial freedom, that this might work...that Marlin may not have to work so hard to make a living.

Marlin and I went Direct in ninety days. That involves acquiring a certain level of new prospects entering into your business as you help those new ones acquire their prospects.

I was particularly good at this venture. I was a people person. With my outgoing, bubbly personality, I believed I could set the world on fire and leave a road for others to follow. I loved helping people.

This business took us all over the country—Texas, Colorado, Utah, Arkansas, and Florida. There were conventions we attended to help us build and increase our knowledge. There were people in place to help you do that also, which were called your up line—

people who had already accomplished a certain level in the business who were there to help you build yours.

This so-called up line is where it gets really interesting. Marlin and I were introduced to people who would change our life— people who made an everlasting impression on how we viewed the world.

The friends we made in Amway are some of the best relationships we have encountered to this day, not that the ones we have established aren't just as important on this journey. But the principles that we learned taught us so much more than building a business. So much more!

We had never really experienced the thrill and excitement of meeting new people, traveling to different places, seeing new sights. There were so many different things to do and learn. I felt I was in the right place, at the right time, with the right people.

I believed God had finally heard me. I had people who looked at me with respect and admiration.

One couple really stood out. About the time Marlin and I were going Direct, they were becoming Emeralds, meaning they had three Directs in their business who had built their businesses to a certain status.

Emerald status is a very respectable position. They had worked hard to help others achieve their goals, while they worked consistently to achieve their own. It really was a win-win situation.

Marlin and I admired this couple for the work we were watching them do for others. Marlin and I always knew what hard work was. Nobody had ever given us anything.

So watching others want to give of themselves to help us achieve our goals was humbling. I knew if I was able to just duplicate them, we would make this business soar. In meeting these new Emeralds for the first time, I knew in my heart that this couple had something special between the two of them. Something I believe I longed for: Mutual respect.

Getting to know them on a personal level was more than what I could have ever dreamed it would be. Ana, a highly sensitive, spiritual soul, gives of herself constantly. Bill, an intelligent and determined gentleman, always makes you feel welcomed. These two would become our dear friends one day; we just didn't know it yet.

After going Direct, there was a trip that we qualified for, and Cancun was the destination. Marlin and I had never been to Cancun, Mexico. This would be a real adventure for us.

There was a large group that we had come to know in this Amway business, and it looked like they had all qualified to bask in the sun down south. But the ones who always seemed to shine were Bill and Ana.

The trip was great. We stayed in a very elite resort where the swimming pool looked out over beautiful blue waters and sparkling sand beaches. You could swim over to the bar, get yourself a cool delight to sip on, then make your way back to the pool's edge and take in the scenery as the waves rolled in. It was breathtaking.

This was *life*. I marveled at the grandeur of God's creation. There were many different places this business would take us—many new faces to meet along the way, and many more relationships to savor.

My heart was full.

As the business grew, obstacles came with it. Growing and stretching one's self to the limit, as you help others climb their mountains, wasn't easy.

At times I felt like I couldn't accomplish this task by myself as Marlin bowed out gracefully more and more. Even though the up line was always there to help, I was standing alone a lot. Marlin was

100 percent dedicated to his harvesting business, as he should be. It was our bread and butter.

There were many times I would go out on my own to show someone this business, and the hours spent away from my family were hard on Marlin and the boys. I was making sure everything was just right at home—that the boys were taken care of with their school. And most important, making sure everything was done for the harvesting business, concerning all the bookwork that needed to be done.

But without Marlin literally by my side supporting me, it was difficult.

There was a point after around three years while I was working hard to establish growth in some of the down line…I came to a stop. I was tired and I needed a break. So I took one. I let Bill and Ana know that it had become too difficult to build this business by myself and that I was letting other things in my life slip away.

They understood, as good friends would. Our friendship never died; it only lay dormant for many years.

I took this down time to spend more time with my family and friends. Shelbey was always a friendly ear, and my buddy Cathy was always ready to put on our gambling shoes and head for Reno. Cathy and Shelbey are two of my closest and dearest friends. And of all things, their birthdays fall on the same day!

I still hadn't spent too much time with my sisters—only at holidays and such. I missed them, but my recovery was much too important. I had been clean seven years, and I was doing the best I knew how to do.

I was no longer using drugs to alter my existence, but I had picked up the horrible habit of smoking cigarettes. Actually, I had started smoking around the time I quit doing drugs. So, basically, I traded one for another, but this one didn't make me high—just still an addict.

It seemed I still needed something to pass the time away—something to do with my hands. You might say take up needlepoint or something—anything is better than polluting your body with toxins. I know all about that, but it seemed like I hadn't lost the yearning to do something you know you're not supposed to do but want to do anyway. I wasn't perfect by any means, but clean.

I read everything I could get my hands on that led me to a higher level of enlightenment. I was in a search mode constantly. I knew I could be better if I just tried harder.

I settled back in and enjoyed being the mother I always loved to be. Graduation was on the horizon for both the boys. A party seemed in order!

And God knows how I love to throw a party. Over the course of the last seven years, I threw lots of parties. I love the idea of putting all my favorite people together and enjoying their company. I'd thrown many, many Christmas parties. The Halloween parties were the funniest, and, of course, I always went all-out for the birthday parties. They were probably the best, and I enjoyed every second, in these precious persons who were given to me. I truly enjoyed watching their eyes light up as they got a taste of all my secret goodies, wanting to know what's in each one.

I was looking forward to watching my sons graduate and giving them a party to let them know how proud I was of both of them.

So, in each passing day, I counted all my blessings and thanked God He had given me such a beautiful life. I had a husband who loved his family and who gave it all; two well-adjusted sons who were both healthy and beautiful; parents whom I came to admire and respect; relationships with my siblings; coming to know peace; real friends—I knew God graced me with their presence.

Who could ask for more? Not me.

God had given me everything.

Marlin's birthday celebration.

I still had some questions that needed to be answered though. It would be difficult to walk through this next phase of my life, but it had to be done. If I were to stay clean, I needed to get all the demons out of my closet. So I prayed to God as to what to do next, and He told me the truth would set me free.

I followed that, but I was to pay a heavy price for that truth. I believe in my heart it was the right thing to do. I picked up the phone and made a call to a man named Daniel.

"Very truly I tell you, whoever believes in me will do the works I have been doing, and they will do even greater things than these, because I am going to the Father. And I will do whatever you ask in my name, so that the Father may be glorified in the Son. You may ask me for anything in my name, and I will do it" (John 14:12-14 NIV).

Chapter 9

Daniel

When I was a little girl, around the age of eight or nine, I remember a picture of a beautiful baby boy who sat upon my grandparents' shelves. I often wondered who this child was but never had the courage to ask.

He was not amongst the sixteen grandchildren. So who was he? There was silence in the air about this boy. I felt it.

In my young mind, I was curious as to why he wasn't talked about, but a picture was worth setting out to admire.

I admired this black and white photo every time I found myself at my grandparents' to visit. I remember standing there looking at his picture as the furnace on the floor blew warm air up on my small body. It felt good.

There was something about him, I whispered to myself, as I asked God, at my tender age, to reveal it to me. Rumors and whispers always caught my attention. At all times I was aware of my surroundings. I knew the truth about this little boy would come out someday. I waited.

I left it at that for years, until one day when I was a young teenager, my cousin Debbie, who was a few years older than me and lived next to my grandparents her whole life, revealed to me a secret.

She told me the picture of the little boy was my half brother, and his name was Daniel. The first question out of my mouth was, "Is he still alive?" As far as Debbie knew, he was.

"How old is he?" I asked. My cousin was more than willing to answer any questions I had. She told me that he was three years older than my firstborn sister. Why were we never told if he's still alive? What happened? I felt betrayed.

Debbie sat me down and told me that my father had gotten a young girl pregnant. He never loved this young lady and had never believed that the child was his since a few different boys had "passed her around" back then, as the story goes, but no one knew the truth. My grandparents didn't care that he didn't want to claim this child, nor did the courts; he was still to give this illegitimate child a last name. So my grandparents and the courts forced my father to marry this young lady in a quick shotgun wedding in Nevada. The two of them never lived together. As soon as they got home, the marriage was dissolved. My father was to pay child support until Daniel was eighteen years of age.

My parents had dated a few times back then, but I don't believe their relationship was serious when all this was happening. Mom was only fifteen at the time. My father did marry my mother three years later. I believe they both fell in love with one another. After they were married they lived with my father's parents for a couple years, until their house was built. My mother became pregnant a few months into their marriage.

I'm sure she was thinking that all she had to do was give my father a son and he would be the happiest person, since he had nothing to do with Daniel. The young woman who had Daniel would bring him over to see his grandparents, and if my father was in the house, he would run out the back door to not get even a glimpse of the child.

This I will never understand. I wondered often how my mother must have felt.

There I was, thirteen or so, now wondering if the reason my father was so mean sometimes was because he never really wanted *us* either—especially girl after girl after girl. Five girls in a row—some not even a year apart! My poor mother; I know she wanted to give him a son.

After hearing this unimaginable story, my life was forever changed. What was I to do with such information? Keep it to myself? Share it with my sisters? I asked God to help me understand it all, because it didn't make any sense to me at all.

Shortly after hearing I had a half brother somewhere out in this world, I met Marlin, and it seemed that God had taken my pain away for a brief moment. My eyes were looking in another direction. Daniel always lingered in my mind; I found myself wondering if he ever thought about us as I thought about him. I decided to keep it to myself for my fear of what would happen to me if my father ever got wind that I knew the truth.

Years went by without a word out of my mouth about it. I was lost in love and lost in a world of my own—a world of resentment, confusion, rebellion, and fear. It was no wonder I chose drugs to deal with my pain; there wasn't anything else to pick from, or so I thought at the time.

With this secret locked up inside of me, I continued to breathe and knew one day I would have the courage to face the reality of confronting my father that I knew about Daniel.

The years went marching by. I'm sure my sisters and I spoke of the possibility that this little boy in the picture could be our half brother, but it was something you really didn't want to talk about.

The day came early in the year 2000—almost thirty years after I learned of Daniel. My search for a higher level of self and the truth had brought me to a place of more confidence than I ever knew possible. I had been clean now for eleven years. And those clean years I spent working on understanding what made me tick—taking me apart piece by piece trying to understand the reasoning of why I was never told the truth…of why I believed I never really mattered, just as Daniel never mattered.

We are human beings, for heaven sakes—not dogs you just give away or kick aside if you don't like them. I felt at the time that I was also kicked aside and then disregarded that we even had a brother.

God had revealed to me that I was to take a stand for the truth. That Daniel was a child of God first, before he was a child of my father's loins. Life is not fair at times—most of the time!—but the truth is always better than a lie, and I shall not run from this truth. It wasn't Daniel's fault he came into this world and began a life knowing that his father never wanted him. I felt Daniel and I shared a bond, even if I had never seen his face.

I called my aunt, who is my father's oldest sister, and asked her if she had an address or telephone number for Daniel. She did. He lived in Modesto, not twenty miles away. She gave me his number, and all I had to do was pick up the phone and call him. I was scared that he might not want to talk to me, but my heart was brave enough to find out.

I made the call.

Daniel answered. "Hello."

"Hello. My name is Bobbett Bettencourt. I hope I'm not bothering you, but do you know who I am?"

"Yes, I do, and you're not bothering me. Thank you for calling. How can I help you?" He's asking me how *he* can help *me?* Who is this calm, gentle voice on the other end of the phone?

"Daniel, I've known about you since I was a little girl and have always been afraid of my father to ask about you. But I'm a grown woman now, who feels she shouldn't have to hide behind my father's shadow. I was wondering if we could meet."

"I would like that. How many sisters and brothers do you have?"

"Four sisters and one brother. Two of my sisters would like to meet you, too. Is that OK?"

"Yes, that's fine. What about the rest?"

"I believe they're not ready, and they actually don't know I've made this phone call to you yet. But they will."

We planned to meet in a few days. We set up a meeting place in Turlock. We said our good-byes, and I'm sure on both parts, we longed to look upon each other's eyes. I would know if he was my father's son with one look.

I called my two youngest sisters and told them all that had taken place. They thanked me for being so brave.

The moment arrived and the instant my gaze fell upon his face, I knew. We knew he was our brother. His eyes were our father's eyes. His lips, his hair, his stature, his hands and fingernails—all were a replica of our father's. He then spoke with a smile and thanked us for thinking of him.

I was thinking to myself what a gentle soul he was and wondering about the people who raised such a pleasant man. Wondering what kind of man he would have been if my father would have wanted him.

But whoever had the honor of raising this man, I commend them for the manner in which they chose to love him. It showed in his character that he was a man of strength.

We enjoyed a wonderful Mexican meal together, telling story after story about the events that brought us to that moment. It was wonderful to know that he thought of us as we thought of him. As we ended our time together, we arranged to meet again.

It was getting close to Easter, so I asked if he would like to come to my house and meet another sister who would like to meet him. He was more than willing. He was going to bring his wife.

I knew this next step was not going to be easy.

Over the course of the next week, I got up enough courage to call my dad and ask him if he would like to have lunch. I believed my father would become angry, and I asked if we could have lunch uptown at one of his favorite restaurants.

When we sat down to order our lunch, I began by telling him about a secret that had been floating around our family ever since I can remember—a secret about a boy named Daniel. This was the first time I ever spoke Daniel's name to my father. The look in my father's eyes was that of resentment and anger—resentment for ever having it happen in the first place and anger that his daughter could even ask him about something that had nothing to do with her. He was trapped, and he didn't like my motives.

But as far as I was concerned, I had no choice. God told me to do this thing for Daniel, not for my satisfaction or my father's. But I knew I had crossed a line in his book.

He looked at me, which seemed like an eternity, and then spoke, "Ask anything you want and then we will never speak about this again."

I asked, "Dad, why were we not told of Daniel?"

"Because it was none of your business. That happened way before you were ever born," he responded.

"I realize that. I was told when I was just a young girl that the picture that sat on your parents' shelf was your son by another woman and that you never wanted him. All of this came from the

Marson's home and mouth. Why were they told this story and not us? We are your children. Are we not important? Our cousins used this boy as a tool to tease and curse all of your children. Dad, please tell me the truth. That's all I want to know."

My father's voice was stern but calm as he begins to tell me that he never believed that the child was his—that the young woman who had Daniel was passed around by a lot of young men. He was told that the child looked like another, not him.

"But why didn't you find out for sure whether he was yours or not?" I asked. "I don't understand why you wouldn't make sure before you cast him out of your life and had nothing to do with him. It's not Daniel's fault he was born into this world."

My father was growing agitated with my questions, but remained composed. He didn't know how to answer my questions, because I believe he had no good answers for me. My father told me that if I was that curious about this man, maybe I should meet him for myself.

"Dad, I already have. We met with him a few days ago. I had to tell you the truth. He looks just like you. Everything is you, copied."

The look in my dad's eyes was shock.

"He's your son, Dad. There is no denying it. He looks just like you." My father didn't have any more words. In his book I had betrayed him, and in mine, he had betrayed me.

I tried to look into my father's eyes as we finished our meal together, but he was not going to let me in. He shut me out.

We still had a twenty-minute ride home to be able to come to some kind of understanding, but it didn't happen. There was silence.

Over the course of the next few weeks I became the black sheep of the family—a bad seed. How could I have done this to my father and mother and to the whole family? I was evil according to my parents and my young brother.

But I wasn't the one who lay with this young woman and got her pregnant. I was an innocent bystander. The truth came to me, and I chose to follow my saddened heart.

The truth is I was in a family who I believed never really wanted *me*. My dad even said he should have never had children. I have learned to accept that fact. It's not that they didn't love me, clothe me, feed me, or shelter me. They just never nurtured me. And I always felt that growing up.

I just *wanted to be wanted*. Children know. They're little people with a heart—more than adults. I was a little girl who wanted nothing more than to love everyone. It didn't come back to me as I wanted it to. I was sad and heartbroken, but I also somehow knew a bigger purpose was at work here.

As time went by, I didn't speak to my parents or my brother for quite some time. I did see Daniel a few more times over the following year and met his family also. Wonderful people. We stayed in contact through e-mails, cards, and letters. The last thing I sent Daniel was a CD of Sarah McLachlan, *Angel*. If you know the words to the song Angel, you'll understand why.

He called and thanked me for the CD and told me that he realized how hard this must have been for my sisters and me and thanked me from the bottom of his heart that we took the time to care and think of him.

That was the last time I spoke to Daniel.

He had a heart attack at his place of work and died at the age of fifty-four. My sister and I attended the funeral. It seemed awkward, but I needed to be there. At the close of the service, as we were walking out, an older woman with tears in her eyes came walking up to us. She had her hands out and took mine in hers.

She asked, "Are you the Bettencourt girls?"

I respond to her plea. "Yes, we are."

"Who is Bobbett?" she asks.

"I am."

Still holding my hands, we start to walk out to the grounds where he was to be laid to rest. She began to tell my sister and me how she loved our father very much. But what we did for Daniel was one of the noblest things that could have possibly been done for him. She continued to tell us that Daniel had told her that meeting us was one of the best things that had ever happened to him. She thanked us over and over again for thinking of him and also for being there in their time of need.

We stood there together and cried, as I told her, "It's the least thing I can do. I wish I could have done more."

She countered, "You've done everything you could for Daniel. God bless you and your family."

One small child being born set a course of events that could no more be stopped than the wind. I love the way God works.

"Get wisdom, get understanding; do not forget my words or swerve from them. Do not forsake wisdom, and she will protect you; love her, and she will watch over you. Wisdom is supreme; therefore get wisdom. Though it cost all you have, get understanding. Esteem her, and she will exalt you; embrace her, and she will honor you" (Proverbs 4:5-8 NIV).

Chapter 10

The Store

It was early in the year 2001 when Marlin and I decided to move in a whole different direction. Not that we would leave the farming business—we added something on top. Earlier, I had mentioned that Marlin was always looking for a better way to make a living. He believed he had.

We had a third-generation relationship with our fuel company, Dickey Petroleum. Marlin had told his friend Danny Dickey, the owner, to keep an eye out for anything that came up for sale in line with a gas station and convenience store.

One day Marlin came home and told me that we need to go look at this store in Atwater. I was a little on the defensive, trying to figure out just who was going to run this thing. I knew he was excited, so I just played along like I always do.

The place needed some work. It wasn't the best location, but it did sit next to a Burger King restaurant. To this day I don't know if that hurt us or not—the burgers there were awful. I ate there approximately *once*.

Well, the price was right for the picking. We dived in headfirst. We didn't know one thing about the gas business. But we applied for the loan, and before we knew it, we were the proud owners of a two-year-old 76 Gas Station and Convenience Store...with car wash included.

Bettencourt's 76 convenience store, 2001.

Some friends and family embraced the idea of us having another business, and some made fun, laughing to our face that we should be wearing turbans. I didn't understand that at the time. But it takes all kinds for this world to go around.

My father and I were on speaking terms again, and I thanked God that he had let me back into his life. But I don't know if he ever truly forgave me for the hurt that I caused him. I prayed that he and my mother and my brother would someday understand why I did what I had to do. Daniel was a real person, with real feelings, and before he was ever born into this world, he was first a child of God.

With that behind us, I gathered enough courage to ask my dad if he would like to help Marlin and me with the opening of the new store—namely, asking some of his hot rod buddies if they would like to bring their custom cars to our grand event. They were more than happy to do so. How they loved to show off their cars. We must have had at least thirty custom cars show up that day to make it the special day it was.

Thank you, Dad.

My dad's pride and joy!!

So we opened with a live radio station blasting, hot barbecue chicken sandwiches, custom hot rods scattered in all directions, and face painting and balloons for the kids! It was smiles all around for the cheap gas!

What a day! It was quite a celebration. We made more money that

My dad and I at our grand opening for the store.

day than any other day I had the store. And boy, did I have the store. It was my baby. I had a lot to learn. But I was open like a book.

I believe I took to the store like a duck to water. My philosophy on this project would be to treat everyone the way I like to be treated and see if I get the same treatment back. It was almost like therapy to me.

I was the boss. What did that mean to me? It meant I had a whole lot of duties I never ventured to even think about before. I've never been the boss before. Now I was staring down at six new faces I'd never seen before, and I got to tell them what to do. There seemed to be a little power in that.

But remember what I told you earlier about a noble manipulation—doing something and knowing you're doing it on purpose. There is noble manipulation just as well as there is evil manipulation. Choose one or the other.

I chose noble. God gave me a heart to care enough about people to help in any way I could. The people that came my way through the store were some of my best moments in life. Coming to know new people on a daily, personal level is not something everyone will experience or want to. I chose to treat my employees with common courtesy and respect. I chose to know them.

Not all, though. Many came and left whom I never knew. But the firstfruits, you might call them…they were special. Brandon, Tammy, April, Tonya, and Marna. Each one was different from the next. I love each and every one of these people. They touched me in a way that changed my life for the better—and forevermore.

Half of them are still in my life today. They are special people and always will be—especially Brandon. What a wonderful friend he was then and still is. I hadn't met very many young men who had his work ethic or the respect that he gave to others every day. Truly a beautiful person, inside and out. If I needed him for anything, he would be right there—and me for him. He is a true blessing that God has graced me with.

There were many challenges to face daily in running a convenience store/gas and car wash. Hundreds of decisions needed to be made day-to-day, almost 24/7. And as always, I handled things with the best grace I possibly could.

As time went along, I got to know each one of my employees and how the daily events of owning and operating a gas station would be played out.

Things were good. Operations were good. Employees were good, at times. I believed that this gas business might be the one thing I needed.

I enjoyed getting up early in the morning and going to work. I had something new to do besides the bookkeeping for our farming business and dealing with my ever-aching back. (I was still going to see doctors and getting a shot in my back to control the pain from that car wreck.)

The months were rolling by fast, and I was starting to get the hang of things when something awful happened to our country.

It was September 11, 2001.

I was getting ready to go to the store and had the morning news on. I happened to look up to the TV, and there were planes flying into some tall buildings! I looked again and saw it was the World Trade Center. It felt like I was living in the twilight zone.

This can't be happening…but it was. I will never forget that day as long as I live. Our country wept.

A brutal force had attacked us, killing thousands. I prayed for the families who had lost their loved ones…and also prayed for the ones who did this. For weeks and months to come it was the only thing that our country could talk about—and for good reason. What the heck was going on?

Life was never the same after that day—especially the gas business. We thought we might have made the biggest mistake of our life buying this store. Time would tell.

The only thing I can tell you about the gas business is it felt like a dictatorship—different state and federal organizations come in telling you what to do, when to do it, and how much it's going to cost.

Large amounts of money ran through my hands, like a big wheel. Every time you thought you might make a few extra dollars, here came another test or compliance upgrade. Oh my word, it became ridiculous.

The fourth year into it, I believed I had all I could take—from customers blaming me for the high gas prices, employee betrayal, theft, vandalism, and upkeep on the store. Plus, I was dealing with a very painful back. I had enough.

At the time, I was taking a lot of pills to cope with going full throttle every day—shots, as many as they could give me, to deaden the pain. My back was a mess.

My plate was full, and I knew it. But I kept going.

I was still doing all the books for M. Bettencourt and Sons. Michael and Mitchell started a new trucking business, which I helped them get started. We were building a new house also, and I was on top of it all. Like I said, my plate was overflowing.

Then a call came with bad news.

It was late in October, 2003. Marlin had just got home from a long day's work from corn chopping, and our son Michael calls us to tell us that he had just been in an accident while returning from one of our job sites.

Some drunk individual ran a stop sign and hit our son broadside. The impact flipped the pickup over that Michael was driving, one complete turn, and then back on its wheels. The other car ended up taking out a few almond trees as he came to a stop in an orchard.

Marlin and I quickly rushed to the scene of the accident three miles from our home to see if our son was OK. He called from his cell phone, so we knew he must not have been hurt too bad. Thank God again.

When we got there, Michael was up on his feet, very upset, and walking around in a daze. The police had just gotten there, and the ambulance was quickly approaching, for I could see the flashing lights coming our way.

I told Michael to sit down and try to relax. We didn't know if he had any internal injuries.

Michael's accident, 2003.

When the ambulance came to a stop, the EMTs quickly came to Michael's side and got him on a stretcher and off to the hospital. When we got to the emergency room, I remember standing by Michael's side, with Amanda his girlfriend on the other. I took his hand and told him that God had protected him and kept him from harm, because he was still to give me grandbabies someday.

Amanda and Michael quickly glanced at one another, for they already knew—and I didn't—that Amanda had a baby growing inside her at that moment!

The doctors checked Michael thoroughly over, and thank the good Lord, he had no internal injuries. That is one of the scariest moments—seeing your child hurt.

A few days went by and I received a phone call from Amanda to let me know that she was pregnant. She was so afraid to make the call to let me know. But I told her everything was going to be OK.

We had a few bumps in the road over the next few months to get this new little life safe and sound to us. God knew that I was going to need this precious beautiful baby boy, more than I have ever needed anything in my life, for what was coming around the corner for me.

My first grandson, who I almost never got to hold, was born to us on May 13, 2004. What a joy this new little guy was to me! Michael and Amanda were living with us at this time, and I was able to bond with this little guy.

We were having a fun time just enjoying this brand-new baby and building our home and doing our business, and then when we least expect it… Another phone call, the kind no one ever wants to receive in the middle of the night. Or ever.

"Not only so, but we also glory in our sufferings, because we know that suffering produces perseverance; perseverance, character; and character, hope. And hope does not put us to shame, because God's love has been poured out into our hearts through the Holy Spirit, who has been given to us" (Romans 5:3-5 NIV).

Chapter 11

Our Loss

My father had been taken by ambulance to the hospital. Something was wrong with his heart. He had what's called an arrhythmia. His heart stopped. The EMTs restarted it.

For six days our family waited to hear the final results from all the testing that was done on his brain. The news wasn't good.

My dad never regained consciousness. He was brain dead. He was hooked up to machines to help him breathe. If we unplugged him, he would surely die.

The family knew that our father, being the proud man he was, would never want to be plugged into any machine to breathe for him. We knew what had to be done. There was no hope.

They disconnected all the tubes that kept him alive. The whole family gathered around his bed and said one more prayer for a miracle and that God's grace, love, and mercy be shed on each one of us as we let go of the one person who taught us almost everything we knew.

I kissed my father good-bye on the forehead…and walked away with the saddest heart I ever knew.

My father labored for three days before his spirit left us. He was pronounced dead on June 13, 2004.

"God is our refuge and strength, an ever-present help in trouble. Therefore we will not fear, though the earth give way and the mountains fall into the heart of the sea" (Psalm 46:1-2 NIV).

Chapter 12

Surrender

This chapter seemed like it would never come. It's been almost a year since I sat down to write. Too many thoughts kept running through my head as to why it just wasn't there. I should know this stuff. Dang, I was the one who lived it.

I prayed to God to please clear my head and mind so that my fingers would somehow dance upon the keyboard again with joy and ease.

The other day I went to my bookshelf looking for an interesting book to read to get me out of this funk...I spotted a title that caught my eye: *A New Earth—Awakening to Your Life's Purpose* by Eckhart Tolle. I pulled it out. I opened the cover and realized that a dear friend of mine, Joyce, had given it to me back in 2006. With all the other choices I had, I never got to it, or—I would like to believe—it wasn't the right time for me to fully bloom.

I read this book with such interest, rereading things over and over so I could understand what the author was talking about.

I now believe I am one of those human beings who has been walking around on the face of this earth sleepwalking and living. I was living with my thoughts in the past or in the future.

I was never totally present. I wasn't living in the *now* and enjoying my life.

In reading this book, a light came on. Now I can see what I didn't see before—being present right this second and watching myself respond to it.

I finally woke up!

Thank you, Eckhart Tolle, for your insight.

It was June 13, 2004. From this day forward, my life would be forever changed.

We laid our father to rest on June 17, 2004. This was the most painful and saddest day in my life, letting go of someone you don't want to let go of.

But, yet, so full of joy too… How can that be?

It was all because of a precious little baby boy named Mason James. I was a new grandma. He blessed us with his presence on May 13. Mason and my youngest son Mitchell share the same birthday. Mason was born one month to the day before my dad took his last real breath. He never got to see Mason before he passed. I wish he could have.

When Michael and Amanda brought this tiny bundle home, they came to stay with us. We had a new baby in the house, and I was so excited I could hardly stand it. We were living in a rental home while our home was being built.

Out at the ranch, we were building our dream home. It sits on a 40-acre piece, right next to our shop and business.

We wanted this home to be special, so we contacted a good friend from our high school years, Manuel Machado. He has a construction company that he runs with his wife and three sons. We knew that he would build us a beautiful home with love and pride, which he did.

Our home is beautiful. Plus, it makes it extra special that his wife, Mary, is a very dear friend. I have known her since birth. We grew up together, for our mothers are very dear friends.

What could be better?

Our good friends, Manuel and Mary Machado and
their three sons, Michael, Jason, and Matt.

So as our home was being built and I was making all the decisions that had to be made each day for that—I was running back and forth from our farming business to the 76 convenience store in Atwater and taking care of all that involved as well. I was also helping Michael get his new trucking business in order and dealing with a bad back and all that involved, but my one true joy was coming home to Mason.

As soon as that baby was in my arms, the grief of losing my father would melt away for a time.

Mason and I bonded together for six months before Michael and Amanda found a place of their own. It was like having my baby Michael all over again. I loved it—checking on him, midnight feedings, diaper changes, and the smell of baby lotion in the air. There is nothing like a new baby to help you heal. I held that baby close and loved on him, for my pain was very deep at the loss of my father.

But I kept going. My mom and siblings seemed to grow apart. Our glue was gone. I grieved the loss of my father alone. My pain was my own.

The next year and a half was a blur—busy with the house, nursing my emotional and physical pain with painkillers and corti-sone cocktail injections every few weeks.

Something had to give…and of all the things it was me. Me? Yes—strong, get-everything-done me.

My body said, "That's enough."

You have to find a way off of this merry-go-round. But I didn't stop. I just kept going. I prayed to God to help me find the courage to stay focused and get everything done. There was no one else who could do it but me, or so I thought…

We moved in January 2006. It was absolutely beautiful—5,500 square feet. It's huge.

Wow, now to get it decorated. This was not a small undertaking. I did my best and made many mistakes along the way.

But by June, I had run out of energy and could no longer function. I found myself on the couch or in bed as much as I could. I had to find an answer.

I went to see a few highly skilled medical doctors, and they told me the same thing—that they would have to cut me from breast-bone to pelvic bone and take all my insides out just to get to the area that needed the attention.

I walked out in tears, thinking no way was I going to allow them to slice and dice me like that. I prayed to God to show me another answer.

And He did.

While surfing the Internet and looking at ways to fix my back without major surgery, I found what I was looking for.

Innovation.

Laser Spine Institute in Florida fixed my back on June 5 with a 4,000 degree laser, and we closed escrow on the sale of the 76 store on June 6. Two things fixed in two days—incredible! I walked out of that hospital two hours after surgery. We stayed in Florida a few days after for the follow-up and then flew home. I had a 12-week recovery.

It was nice not to have the store to manage or to think about. It was time to heal. It was hard to stay still, but I knew how important it was to follow the doctor's orders—especially since Marlin and I were going to be grandparents again! I needed to get well so I could have no problem holding my grandsons or playing with them.

My oldest son, Michael, and his wife Amanda, were getting ready for baby number two. Marshall David would be blessing us with his arrival on July 14, 2007.

It had been a year since my back surgery—everything seemed to be going much smoother. No more pain, but my emotional state of mind was far from well.

It was a day in October while I was getting ready to go into town to a local upholstery shop. We had only been in our new home for ten months. I should be on the top of the world. My back was fixed, I had two beautiful grandsons, and no more store to run every day. I also had a husband and sons who loved me more than anything.

I had just gotten out of the shower when it hit me. Wrapped in only my towel, I fell to the floor in a heart-wrenching cry. "Lord, hear me! I can't do this anymore. I need Your help. I'm lost and lonely and don't know where to turn. Please take this heavy heart and give me peace!"

I don't know how long I stayed on the floor praying and crying, but when I looked up, there was my little dog, Molly. She was sitting there staring me straight in the eyes. She licked my face, as if to tell me everything was going to be OK.

I believe I had a nervous breakdown or God was trying to get my attention. I didn't tell anyone. It was between me and Molly and God.

I got up, got ready, and went to town. As I walked into the shop, I started looking around. They were busy. But this one woman came up to me and asked if I needed any help. I started to tell her my needs, about this one ottoman that hadn't turned out very well and needing it redone.

I really couldn't tell you how we started talking about God and Jesus. But there we were sitting at this table, material samples and people all around, and it was like we were in our own world, just the two of us, expressing our thoughts to one another about God. Now that just doesn't happen to me. I don't think it ever had before.

God answered my prayer. I knew it driving home. He put someone on my path to help me find my way again. Her name is Lupe—a beautiful Mexican woman. She has gorgeous eyes and dark soft skin. She looked like an angel, and to this day I believe she was one for me.

She helped me get my house together after another decorating company almost totally ruined it. That was an expensive mistake but a whole other story. I'm not going there.

It was getting close to Christmas, and I had asked Lupe if she would like to help me decorate for Christmas. Of course, she said yes, and for the next few days we really got to know each other. We talked a lot about God and Jesus. I had told her that I had already read the Bible a few times. I had accepted Christ into my life but was not attending any church. I had done all that, and it really wasn't for me. I was just living my life, trying to be a good person, loving others, helping when I could, and praying when I needed God to help me.

She asked me this: "How's that going for you?"

I stared at her, "Well, not very good."

She said, "Can I tell you something?"

"Certainly."

She's said, "The Word is alive."

"What do you mean?"

She said, "When you read God's Word, it is alive. The Bible is a living entity. When you read His Word and know His Word, God will show Himself to you in ways you do not understand yet. He will help you heal and find peace."

I didn't understand exactly what she meant. "You mean to tell me that if I read the Bible, I will be able to have peace in my mind and not feel so sad and afraid all the time?"

She said, "Yes."

"OK," I said. "I will accept that challenge. I will read every day. I will pray and seek God and Jesus. I pray that you are right. I want you to be right with all my heart. I'm so very tired."

I read and earnestly sought the Lord for the next eight months. All I can say is…

She was right.

I found a peace and a truth to live by. I love all Jesus' principles and teachings about life —especially the one about sowing and reaping. Give and it will be given. Love each other. Give love!

God had a plan that day for Lupe and me to meet and to become friends through the power of the Holy Spirit. All praise goes to our King in heaven for His abiding love and the grace He shares with everyone who seeks Him. I knocked on the door, and He opened it—and sent Lupe! She is a dear friend and always will be.

I was becoming one of God's best students. I couldn't get enough—so much that I even started looking at a few churches. I got involved with a Bible study group.

But it didn't click until late in August 2007 when my brother invited me to a church about thirty minutes from where I live. Actually, the pastor there is my sister-in-law's cousin. I met him once a few months earlier at her aunt's funeral. So with my brother's invitation, I went.

It was a Pentecostal church. I knew it was going to be a little loud and crazy, but I had been to one of these churches before. I loved the worship—very open and honest and reverent.

I walked in and found a seat in the back. It's a small, humble church. Maybe fifty people tops adorned the seats. I felt comfortable...until after the singing and worship were over.

Pastor Ralph steps up to the podium, looks out to his congregation and says, "Bobbett, could you come up here please?"

What? *Me?* You're calling me up to the front? In front of everyone?

I turn to my brother and say, "What's this about?"

He shrugged his shoulders as if to say, "I don't know." OK...

I walk to the front. Here in front of me stands a 6'3" or taller, big man of God staring down at me. I feel three inches tall.

He whispers to me only, "I see a mighty long line behind you."

In my naive way, I turn to see who is behind me. As I turn back around, he has his finger wagging back and forth, and he says to me, "The Lord has asked me to give you a message."

"He has?" I ask in total bewilderment.

"Yes, you will bring many to Christ."

"I will?"

"Are you ready, Bobbett?"

A thousand thoughts rush through my head. I feel almost dizzy. My whole life flashes in front of me—all the things I'm guilty for. I'm an addict. I killed my unborn child. I had hurt so many loved ones…

I don't deserve to be forgiven, I think. Why is God calling me? I'm not good enough to do this kind of work.

Then I remember all the disciples from the Scriptures. None of them were good enough. God picks the weakest link to set His plans in motion. He had found me. He heard my prayer.

But, really—*me?* If you only knew! I'm the weakest one of all! An addict.

But who am I to question God?

I look up into the pastor's face and say with tears in my eyes, "Yes, I think I am."

"OK, Bobbett. Get ready."

Now, as I stand there, in front of this man of God who's had a Bible clutched under his arm since the age of ten, he places both his hands on the top of my head.

Then he speaks loudly. It sounds like a roar—powerful.

"Congregation, we're going to pray for Bobbett today. The Lord has given her a mighty work. She is going to need all the courage and strength to get through what is about to be revealed. Let's pray.

"Thank you, Lord, for Your servant Bobbett. You have called her into Your kingdom. She will touch many hearts in the love she has to give through You, our Lord and Savior Jesus Christ. She is called to bring glory to Your name. Praise Your holy name, Jesus Christ...."

As Pastor Ralph continues to pray over me, I feel my body go warm, like someone pouring hot oil over my head. I feel tears running down my face; my whole body is quivering. I feel more peace than I had ever known in my life. It is not from this earth. It is powerful, but yet so gentle—something not known to me.

The Holy Spirit had come and touched me. This is the only explanation I can come up with. That was not me.

This is when everything came to a single truth for me. When you know, you know, you know. There is a greater power than ourselves who holds all things together.

It's *beyond* whatever we could imagine. This God who created the cosmos and us in it, loves us. He loves us so much He sent His only begotten Son to show us what true love is and then to go to a cross to die a horrible death for us. He died for us so that we might be saved through His blood. The ultimate sacrifice.

He knew what He had to do. He was sent for that very reason. He was here to bring love and compassion and show us humility. He came to die. But more than that, He was raised from the dead by the power from our Father in heaven.

And now He is seated at the right hand of the Father. Glory be to Your name!

Jesus Christ.

After the pastor prayed for me, I got back in my seat. I don't remember walking back, but I was there. I sat there stunned at what just happened.

That was an out-of-body experience.

As I was filtering all this, I felt a small shove on my shoulder coming from my left. It was a little southern eighty-year-old woman—my sister-in-law's grandma. She passed her hand over my brother's shoulder to get to me.

She looked at me square in the eyes and asked, "What did He say to you?"

With a shrug of my shoulder, I said modestly, "I'll bring many to Christ." Almost like a question.

She sits back in her seat and says, "I've been coming to this church for thirty years, and I've never seen that yet. Praise be to God."

I just sat there. I had already thought maybe this might just be an every Sunday occurrence. But I guess not.

This was just the beginning to what God had in store for me that day. When you say, "I'm ready," you better be ready to go to work, because I was on call!

I got home and the first thing I did was to call Marlin. We were in corn season, so he was chopping. "Marlin, you are never going to believe what happened in church today."

He said to me, "You're never going to believe what happened to *me* today!"

OK. He's got my full attention now. "What?"

Marlin continued, "Sammy was walking through the shop this morning, and she stopped to ask me a question. She asked if we would still be willing to help Angelo, because she doesn't know what to do anymore."

I asked, "What's wrong with him?"

Two weeks earlier he had come back to work for us after a year of running his own company. We knew he had been struggling to stay clear from alcohol. He had been staying with his brother-in-law in the city for the past few months getting his head straight. Marlin and I knew that it would be a risk to hire him back, but we also believe everyone needs a second chance. So we did.

Corn chopping started as usual, but before Angelo's first day back ended, he fell off the chopper—ten feet to hard concrete and dirt. He broke his arm and was pretty much done for the season.

Now, Sammy, his wife, was still driving a truck for us every day. So when she got home every night she was walking into her home to someone who was lost in his mind… He was incoherent…no reasoning…not making any sense…depressed and feeling very sorry for himself…lost…very lost in a sea of deep despair.

He had lost his business, he was losing his wife and respect from his children, and now just lost his job and income. This man needed help or he was going to die.

This is where I come in, but really… It's where God comes in and takes control.

After hearing about Angelo, I proceeded to tell Marlin about the awesome experience I had in church, and the first thing out of his mouth was, "I guess this one's for you, babe!"

After church, I was going over to my brother's home to celebrate a birthday. I told Marlin I would stop over at Angelo's and check on him. When I got there, I knocked at the door. No one answered. I told myself I would stop by on my way back home, which I did.

This time Sammy's Mom answered the door. "I'm here to see Angelo."

She said, "I don't think you want to see him, Bobbett. He's really bad."

I looked her in the eyes and said, "I believe that's why I'm here."

She led me back to his bedroom, turned, and left.

What I witnessed was someone who was not there mentally…a hollow shell…a tormented mind…twisted and not making any sense…groaning with agony from his gut as he lay on his bed, filthy from not showering.

This is when the Holy Spirit showed up in full strength. I had never in my life ever prayed out loud in front of *anyone*. I was even embarrassed to say grace over a dinner table. But there I was…

I went over to him and knelt down by the side of his bed, gently placed my hands on this trembling body, and started to pray. I asked our dear Lord, *"If it be Your will, please save Angelo. He is a good man who's made some bad decisions, as we all have. Give us strength and courage now and faith to see this through."*

I then started speaking a language I had never heard before, and I didn't understand what I was saying either. But I continued to pray as the Lord prayed through me.

The power was so overwhelming, I sat there and just wept!

I didn't know it at the time and neither did Sammy or the family, but Angelo had been drinking rubbing alcohol and sniffing gasoline just to get a buzz. This is on top of the pain pills and sleeping pills the doctor prescribed him for his broken arm. Angelo was on his way out.

But God was going to show Angelo and me how real He is…that this is not just an illusion…that there is nothing to be afraid of…that His glory and everlasting Word have the power to heal.

I laid my head on the side of the bed where I could see Angelo's face. As he was curling over in pain, he said so softly, "You're an angel."

I kissed his hand and said, "Maybe today, Angelo, maybe today."

I stayed with him for a few hours. Got him cleaned up and walked him outside for some fresh air. We decided to go for a drive with the windows down and Christian music playing in the background. It was a clear, hot August night. The stars were shining brightly, and I knew that God had intervened in what we had just experienced.

I got back to Angelo's and put him to bed. He was very weak, but the fresh air did him good. I told him I would be back in the morning and that I was going home to find a place for him to go and start treatment for his alcoholism. He told me no, that he was not going anywhere. He told me that a few times, and finally I told him that if he doesn't go, he would surely die.

With him still shaking his head no, I left.

I went online and found a place close by to take him in the morning. No problem. All ready to go! But little did I know, God had others plans…

I wake the next morning, knowing today's events are going to be interesting and unpredictable. I'm standing in front of the mirror drying my hair, contemplating how this day would turn out, when all of the sudden it feels like hot oil has been poured over my head—just like I had felt in church the day before.

I hear in my head a voice that says, "You're not taking Angelo anywhere."

Now I'm confused. Why would I think of that? "I am going to take Angelo to a treatment center," I say to myself.

The voice again repeats itself: "You're not taking Angelo anywhere."

"Yes, I am. I'm taking him to get help."

"No, you're not. Trust and have faith. You have everything he needs—your love and his trust, your experience, and, most of all, your time. You're taking him home with you."

"*I am?*"

I can't believe what had just occurred.

But I do believe…and will never question God's abilities. I thought I was talking to myself for a minute, until you know when you know that you know that it wasn't you making the decisions any longer.

I finished getting ready, praising God the whole way through. I called my office and asked my assistant to please come over and clear the bar of all alcohol. Then I called Marlin and told him how God had spoken to me this morning.

He couldn't believe it either. It was like a big fat elephant in the room. You could not ignore the power that was moving through us at this time. It was awesome!

I went to go get Angelo. He had no idea what was about to happen. I walked into his bedroom and got him up. He was a little better but not much. I asked if he was ready to go and he told me no and that he wasn't going.

Cleverly, I say, "Angelo, there is no arguing about this. You are going. I have found the best place in sixteen counties."

He glared into my eyes as if to say, "No way." I looked back into those sad, weepy eyes and told him, "God has told me to take you home with me. So let's get ready."

He started crying deep sobs of appreciation, saying over and over, "Thank you, thank you, thank you. You are my angel."

"Maybe today, Angelo, maybe today."

Angelo stayed with us for three weeks. The first week was to detox and the other two to start his journey being sober and learning how much Christ loves him. He had never even opened a Bible or read any Scriptures in the forty-five years he's been breathing.

God had a plan. And He used me to help Him carry it out. All I ever wanted to do was to help others in any way I could—especially when addictions are thrown in the mix.

Angelo thought he *was* his addiction. He thought he was worthless. But God came in and turned the whole thing into one of the most positive and heartfelt stories that has ever been told.

God woke Angelo up. He knows now what the most important thing in life is: love. It's the love you give to others and the love that God gives us. There is nothing else.

Angelo accepted Christ into his life the first week he was with us, and the rest is beautiful history. Five years later, Angelo is still working for us and is still clean. He leaves his devotional in the tractor so he can stay close to God's Word.

All I can say is that being used for the glory of God is the most awesome feeling! There is nothing finer than watching someone else's life literally being transformed in front of your eyes.

Angelo and me.

"'For I know the plans I have for you,' declares the Lord, 'plans to prosper you and not to harm you, plans to give you hope and a future. Then you will call on me and come and pray to me, and I will listen to you. You will seek me and find me when you seek with all your heart. I will be found by you,' declares the Lord, 'and will bring you back from captivity'" (Jeremiah 29:11-14 NIV).

Chapter 13

My Will Meeting God's

The holidays were quickly approaching, and I felt peace and harmony in my soul. God had shown me a miracle—a miracle of healing. My faith had become stronger than ever before. I knew beyond a shadow of a doubt that God was real and that He was in control.

We never expected such a great harvesting season that year, but as always, we gave thanks to the Lord. When you open your heart to others and live a life of sowing, you shall reap a harvest.

If anyone should know this, it would be a farmer's wife. I had watched Marlin sow and give to others his whole life. My man is a man of heart and has nothing but goodwill for others. He strives always to do his best for himself, his family, his business, and others. I am so blessed to have him for my partner, friend, and husband.

I never wanted to be with anyone but him—my soul mate.

The good Lord was about to reveal something else to me that would change the whole course of my life and send me into full service for Him.

As the new year rolled around to 2008, Marlin and I made plans to visit some dear friends in Concord, California. It was the third week in January—the 19th to be exact. We were going to drive up the coast and stay the weekend at their coastal home. But a few days earlier, my daughter-in-law Amanda got very sick. She had been getting sick off and on over the past three years.

My handsome husband, Marlin, at Bill and Ana's coastal home.

I was on my way back from town when Amanda called me on my cell phone. I could hardly understand what she was saying. But what I did hear was, "Bobbett, I can't move! I can't move! I can't get out of bed—it hurts too bad...."

I said, "I'll be right there."

When I got there, I asked her what she had been taking for the pain. She handed me a bag of pills that a specialist prescribed for her. She was diagnosed as having rheumatoid arthritis. She had been taking a pain pill so strong that you could call it a legal form of heroin—and a whole array of other different drugs! I just couldn't believe it.

I had no idea she was taking all that medicine. I knew she was struggling but didn't know it was from prescribed medicine. She had been taking it all for over three years.

She was a very sick little lady.

Amanda is five-foot nothing and weighs maybe all of a hundred pounds. A tiny little petite Korean gal, she's as cute as a button. She had nothing left to fight with. I believe she was very close to death. We got her to emergency, but the hospital was really no help. Marlin and I didn't know what to do.

We called our friends, Bill and Ana. We told them what was going on and that we didn't know if we should leave under the circumstances. They sincerely felt empathy for Amanda but desperately still wanted us to come up.

They then told us about a product that they had been drinking called MonaVie. They believed that whatever Amanda was dealing with, this product would certainly help and not hurt. MonaVie is loaded with nutrients, something her body could surely use.

Our friends would not steer us in the wrong direction; we trusted them with all of our hearts! We got in the car and drove two hours to get some of this juice for Amanda.

On our way back home, we called Michael to see how Amanda was doing. He had taken her again to the emergency room. Still they were not able to help her. So, with Michael on his way back from the hospital and us with juice in hand, we rushed back to start feeding Amanda this product and just prayed to our awesome Lord that somehow, someway this would make Amanda feel better.

As the weeks went by, we did see a little improvement. She was able to get out of bed and take care of her boys a little. Mason was now four and Marshall was two.

These two little guys are full of energy and always on the move. Thank God for our precious Kayla, who is twelve. She is Amanda's firstborn.

My granddaughter Kayla is very close to her brothers. She has been a caretaker for these two little ones ever since Mommy started to get sick, back in 2004. So Kayla has been mommy number two.

All I can say about my grandchildren is that they have my whole heart. I love them more than life itself, and I truly see these little people for who they are.

I look deep into their eyes, and they know Grandma loves them and that they can trust me with all of their hearts.

I love all my grandchildren the same, but I do have a very strong bond with Mason. We just click together!

Now, Marshall is only two; I'm sure we're going to click together someday also. But Mason was the one in my arms as I grieved the loss of my father. This bond is tight, as is the bond with Mason's father, Michael.

And Kayla—I got to meet this precious little cupcake when she was just seven. So, now at twelve and as beautiful as can be, I have watched her become a young lady. What a treat! I

My precious Mason and me.

always wanted a daughter. And when Amanda married my son, I got two daughters. How awesome is that?

There is one other little guy. His name is Lukas, and he's nine.

Lukas is Amanda's second born. Amanda does not have primary custody of Lukas, so we don't get to see him as much as I would like to. With Amanda being sick a lot, it was just too hard to try to arrange more visits with him.

With the improvement that we were seeing with Amanda, Marlin and I decided to go ahead and continue with our travel plans. We were going to Hawaii on February 12 with some great friends, Albert and Lana.

So, here we were basking in the sun, umbrella drinks in hand, and enjoying all that Hawaii has to offer with our wonderful friends when Marlin's cell phone rang. It was Bill and Ana Erb telling me that I needed to go online and check out my online office, all provided by MonaVie. There was an opportunity to build a huge business—all by sharing this product.

I asked, "What are you talking about?"

I really wasn't interested in getting involved with another network marketing company at the time and trying to build anything. I just wanted my daughter-in-law to get better. So, I was as polite as I could be and told them that when I got back home I would certainly check it all out.

And, since I gave them my word that I would, one of the first things I did when we got home was call Bill and Ana so I could get the information I needed to access my MonaVie office. I went on the site and saw that there were over seventy people in my business. Now, how could that be? I never even enrolled anyone.

A few days passed, and I went back online to check it out again, only for curiosity purposes…and now there were over one hundred people in our business.

I called Bill and Ana back and asked, "What is this all about?"

They told me, "This is the most amazing thing we've ever seen. It's a berry from the Amazon—loaded with nutrition. MonaVie is only three years old and already doing millions of dollars of business. All you have to do is share the product with others and enroll them with a membership and let them get their own juice. You don't have to buy a bunch of product. They buy their own product all online. Then you get compensated for bringing new distributors into the business."

They were so excited. I was excited for them, but…

I told them that I was in the middle of writing my book and would really like to get it finished. I didn't think I had time for anything else in my life right then. With our farming business, my grandkids, and getting the book done, I didn't think so… They totally understood. I thanked them for sharing the juice with us for Amanda's sake and for the business opportunity. But I was going to pass for now.

But the thing is, God had already put into work what was in store for me. My heart was being tugged on, big time. I felt like God was telling me to look into this. There was something there. So every time I would go to the computer to sit and write, I found myself on the MonaVie site, looking at who was behind this product. I researched what made it different from anything else out there. Believe me when I say, I did my due diligence.

And since Amanda was doing better…I called Bill back.

"OK," I said, "what do I have to do to start this MonaVie thing?"

He said, "All you have to do is tell others what this juice is doing for you and Amanda and let them decide if they would like to try it for thirty days. Then enroll them with a membership for $39.00 and help them order their juice."

"Well," I said, "that's too easy. Is that it?"

"That's it," he said. "Then you'll get paid."

"Oh, really?"

Now the money part wasn't really my concern. I guess that would be a by-product of a good product. I just wanted others to be able to experience what this juice had to offer. As always, I just wanted to help others.

So, that is what I did. I enrolled twenty-five people in less than two weeks, and I was on a roll. I told everybody about it. Some did, some didn't. It didn't make any difference to me. I just promoted, and I went to what's called Diamond in ten months. Diamond is $200,000 a year. To say the least, I was excited for all the possibilities.

Amanda and I riding the wave for MonaVie, 2010.

It is so true—you are who you hang out with. As I was traveling to different conferences for MonaVie, I was introduced to a great group of people who were more than willing to take their time and energy and help me succeed. Their first thoughts are how they can serve others. I love that.

I was able to spend some quality time with some of these great leaders and learn from them, when Marlin and I were rewarded with a trip to Hawaii in September 2009 for going Diamond.

MonaVie put us up at the Grand Wailea in Maui. It was absolutely breathtaking. We had the best time getting to know others and taking in the sights. I love the people I have met in MonaVie. I've come to know some wonderful individuals, and you know who you are.

This company is exceptional. All the right people and elements have come together to make this company a huge success. I thank God every day that I'm a part of something that is changing the face of the planet.

The principles that the founder, Dallin Larsen, lives by are God first, family second, and business third. There is no way you can fail with that foundation in place.

So I dug in and learned as much as I could about how the network marketing business works and the company that manufactures this product. I was amazed and overwhelmed at how big this company is.

MonaVie has grown every day since they launched in 2005 and is growing still. They ranked eighteen in the top Five Hundred in *Inc. Magazine* as one of the fastest growing companies in 2009. Simply amazing.

I feel very blessed.

I was working my MonaVie business and still doing the books for our farming operation, which I have done for the last thirty years.

God had put on my heart that it was time to make a change. With all the traveling I was doing with MonaVie, I asked Marlin if it would be possible to hire someone to do the books so I could pursue my MonaVie business and finish this book. He thought it was a good idea, and it just so happened that my sister Benni was looking for a job at the time. She has twenty years experience working for another company. I knew she would be an asset to ours. Plus, I trust her like I trust myself.

And, like I said earlier in the book, Benni and I are like peas and carrots. We just go together. It was so nice to have her back in my life every day. Knowing that she would be stepping into my shoes, so to speak, was a comfort.

So in November 2009, I hired Benni and started the training process. There was so much to learn. But I was confident she could do it.

The holidays were here again, and I was so excited to see some of my time being freed up. 2010 was going to be a great year. Marlin and I were very excited about Mitchell and Leslie's new little bundle of joy, who was on its way. He would be here some time in March. With all the joy we were having with our family, it was so difficult to watch so many people lose everything.

The economy was struggling like I had never seen it before. The housing market crashed over the last two years, and everything seemed to slow to a snail's pace. So many people were out of work. There were no jobs anywhere.

So, when people are hurting, what do you do? I tried to do my best and offered them a wonderful opportunity to build their own business, all by sharing this amazing product. And as more business owners start building their own businesses, the economy grows. Every one of us has a part to play in the big scheme of things.

We are really all one. People helping people—spiritually, financially, and physically.

So yes, 2010 was going to be a great year. Or so I thought...

In the first part of February, I started to feel off balance just a little. Then one night when I stepped out of bed to use the bathroom, I fell. I tried to get up, but everything was spinning out of control. I was so dizzy I thought I was going to be sick. I finally got up and made my way to the bathroom, but I had to cover my eyes so the room wasn't going round and round. I lay down in the bathroom and started to pray to God.

"Father, please help me. What is going on?" I just lay there, trying not to be scared.

But I was. I started thinking the worst, of course. Maybe I needed to see a doctor. This has never happened to me before. I'm the one who doesn't even get headaches.

As I made my way back to bed, I prayed this would be gone in the morning—but it wasn't.

When I got to the doctor the next day, he told me that he thought it must be vertigo. He prescribed me some pills to stop the dizziness, but even then, I was in bed for over a week.

When I was able to get back to the office to start training Benni again, I couldn't concentrate anymore. She sent me home. I had forgotten who I even spoke to in the last week. My memory was gone. My ability to reason and function wasn't there. I was struggling. I started to push everyone away from me—especially all my MonaVie friends. I didn't want to speak to anyone. This lasted for nearly four months.

Whatever happened to me was not good. I couldn't think right anymore. My confidence was shattered into tiny bits. There was no way I could face others like this.

I prayed every day for a healing. For if I don't have my brain to help me accomplish all the things I want to do, then what?

By September, I was a wreck. I wasn't feeling well almost every day. My whole body hurt, and I knew I needed to do something to stop this. I knew the juice was doing its part with my nutrition, but my head was doing something entirely different.

I finally went to my chiropractor to see if I needed an adjustment.

And as I was sitting in her office, I broke down and started crying. I told her what had happened to me. She suggested I go see a wellness doctor—she wanted to help, but it was out of her hands.

So that's what I did.

I had lost all confidence in the medical industry and wanted nothing to do with a doctor that was going to try and give me pills—not after what they did to Amanda.

After a long consultation and eight vials of blood later, this doctor was able to find my problem. My adrenal glands were not working. They had shut down. My stress level was off the charts. My hormones were all messed up, and most definitely so was my head.

With the right supplements, diet, exercise, and time, my body was starting to heal, and I grew in confidence that this doctor was going to be able to get me back where I wanted to be: a: strong confident woman again.

I gathered up enough courage to go to a MonaVie event that was coming to Sacramento at the end of October. I hadn't done much with MonaVie for a long time. It was going to be a great time with Amanda, my Kayla, Benni and her daughter, Melanie, and my mom. We planned to stay the night, have a nice dinner, and then go to the conference the following day.

I was so excited.

The next day I was able to see all my MonaVie friends. One in particular, Cheryl Henderson, whom I met through R3Global, a training system that enables distributors to plug in and become successful in building a network business, all designed by Brig and Lita Hart. She and her husband Ed are the directors for New Life Network Ministries. They have traveled with Brig and Lita for over twenty-eight years, helping thousands of people come to terms with whatever is ailing them, all with love and prayer. She's a beautiful woman filled with the power of the Holy Spirit. I just love her.

She told me that she and Ed had just written a book and it would be out soon. I was so excited for her. They both have so much to give.

So, naturally when she told me about her book, I told her about mine.

The first thing she said was, "I need to introduce you to John Mason."

I said, "Really?"

I was like a kid in a candy shop, for I had just enjoyed listening to him on stage. He was one of the speakers that weekend for the conference. He is a man full of God's wisdom and he has the gift to deliver it! John sends out a strong message to be the original person God intended you to be. Don't settle for anything less. Don't look back. Look forward and decide today to take steps toward His plan for your life.

First Thessalonians 5:24 KJV says, "Faithful is he that calleth you, who also will do it."

John's message is everything I'm about. I couldn't wait to meet him!

It was getting late in the afternoon, and we were going to be leaving soon, but I hadn't gotten to meet John yet. I just said a little prayer right there in my chair—that if it's meant to be, it will be so, and I left it like that. I gathered my things up and got the girls ready to go.

I'm heading out the door and walking over to my hotel on the other side of the street when who do I spy walking about ten feet in front of me? John Mason.

God is so awesome! He literally set this up for me.

But I have to be brave and call out his name—which I do. I wasn't going to let an opportunity like this slip away!

"John," I call out. He hesitates a bit, then continues walking very fast. I call his name again, even louder this time. "JOHN!"

He stops and turned to see who this crazy lady is yelling for him in the streets of Sacramento.

I catch up with him and introduce myself. He said, "You're the little lady that Cheryl told me about."

"Yes, I am."

"I hear you wrote a book."

"Yes, I did."

He asks, "What is the title?"

"Who Am I Anyway?" I answer.

"Nice title. What's it about?"

"Addiction, recovery, discovery, and surrender."

"Here is my card. Please send it to me, and we'll go from there."

Surprised and overwhelmed, I managed to get out the biggest thank you ever. "When I get home, I'll send it to you."

I'm sure I was grinning ear to ear, thinking about all the possibilities.

My book was in its rawest form. I wrote it from the deep, core places of my heart and gut. It was not an easy book to write. I was writing about truths—truths that some might not want to hear about.

But somehow, God kept telling me to write this story. There is someone who needs to hear it.

So, on faith, I continued, knowing that God had His hand on the whole thing and that there is nothing to be afraid of anymore. For the truth will set you free from the bondage of fear.

And this brings us back to the title of this book.

Who am I anyway?

I do believe I am the essence of all our Creator has created. Simply put, a being of energy and light, believing there is no separateness. We are all the same stuff, but in many different forms.

I am here to bring love and compassion to everyone I meet, without judgment. I'm not perfect by any means—no one is—but I try like there is no tomorrow to be what God has called me to be!

A servant.

I hear God's voice in the stillness.

"Be still, and know that I am God" (Ps. 46:10 NIV).

When I look up into the night sky, I marvel at the thought of a perfect sphere flowing in a vast sea of stars. And to think that all mankind, for thousands of years, has been walking on the face of this big blue marble in outer space! And we are all just trying to do the same thing—survive upon it. It boggles my mind.

We all want peace. It's a common link between us all.

So every day I would look in the mirror at myself and ask these questions:

Who am I?

Why am I here?

Dear Lord, if it be Your will, will You please reveal this to me? I'm lost and feel like I'm not home in my own skin.

I must have asked God those questions thousands of times over the span of my life.

God *did* answer me, for He is faithful. He has always been with me. He was always telling me who I was and how much He loved me. I just wasn't listening closely enough. I needed to be still so I could hear Him.

My mind moves very fast. So in looking back on everything that has happened in the past few years, I realized why God put me down to my knees with dizziness. I learned patience and to be still so I could hear Him clearly whisper to me, "Bobbett, I love you. I Am here with you always. I will give you whatever you need. Seek Me and all will be given unto you."

Oh, I'm listening now.

I know now the purpose that God has for me.

There are no more questions.

There is no more fear.

I give praise to our Father in heaven, for He heard my cry and healed my pain. My will met God's.

Forever I am Yours!

So, who am I anyway?

I am the one who has made peace with the present moment.

The *now*.

I'm the positive side of the negative. I'm the one making a conscious choice every day to always see the positive in everyone and everything!

I no longer give much thought to the past or the future. I just move every day to serve and in that, I am one with *life*. Being one with life is being one with the *now*. I've realized that I don't live my life, but Life lives through me. Life is the dancer, and I am the dance.

My life is about service, caring for others, and unconditional love, which is true love.

Ask yourself: What is my life about?

I do believe you are exactly who you need to be, at exactly the right time you're living it. You are who you are and no one else.

So, no one else can tell you who you are but you and God. So don't let them.

You do have the ability to achieve whatever you desire.

Every one of us has value—precious value. This is why Christ died for you—because you hold so much value. I believe we were put here to acknowledge His sacrifice for us and to help others realize this also. I have come with acceptance and surrender to it all. My way was too painful. God's Holy Word and precious Lamb is the only way I want to live.

The truth of true love is sacrifice—Christ's sacrifice to you and me and everyone.

He loves you that much!

We sacrifice every day with everyone we know…for love. God set it up that way, and no one's changing it. You can't. It would be impossible.

You can go against it if you like. But what I found when I wasn't living a lifestyle of Christ's principles was that my life was in turmoil.

So today I surrender it all to Him again, my Eternal, Almighty Father! I know You love me and everyone else more than life itself. For You are Life forever!

It's hard, but yet so simple, when you surrender and let go of pride and ego.

My prayer is that you find a healing in my story, as much as it healed me to write it.

Bettencourt family, 2010.

The Prayer of Jabez

And Jabez called on the God of Israel saying,
"Oh, that You would bless me indeed,
And enlarge my territory,
That Your hand would be with me, and
That You would keep me from evil,
That I may not cause pain!"
So God granted him what he requested.
1 Chronicles 4:10

Author Contact Information

To purchase books or for more information, please contact:
Bobbett Bettencourt
P. O. Box 819
Hilmar, CA 95324

Websites:
www.whoamianyway.com
www.linkedin.com/pub/bobbett-bettencourt/38/20b/449

E-mail:
whoamianyway2012@aol.com

Facebook & Twitter:
www.facebook.com/pages/Who-Am-I-Anyway-
Bobbett-Bettencourt/116999578411174
www.twitter.com/bobbett58